Python Progr for Beginners

A Step-by-Step Guide to Learn Basics, Functions, Modules and Much More

By

HARLEY HANSEN

Table of Contents

Introduction

Python is a popular high-level programming language that can be used for various tasks due to its interpretive nature, object-oriented design, and dynamic semantics. One probably uses something powered by Python every day without even realizing it.

Python was initially released on February 20, 1991, and was written by Guido van Rossum. While individuals may be familiar with the python as a large snake, the Python programming language derives its name from a classic BBC television comedy sketch series titled Monty Python's Flying Circus. The fact that Python was created by just one person is one of its most impressive qualities. Copyright restrictions make it difficult, if not impossible, to publicly acknowledge the contributions of the many individuals who work behind the scenes at the major corporations that often develop and publish new programming languages. Python is not like this.

None of Python's components were created or refined by Guido van Rossum alone. While thousands of often anonymous programmers, testers, users (many of whom aren't IT specialists), and enthusiasts have contributed to Python's rapid global adoption, it is clear that Guido's mind was the source of the original inspiration. The Python Software Foundation is a community of developers, programmers, and users who work together to improve and promote Python and its ecosystem.

Python is everywhere, and people use many gadgets powered by Python every day, whether they know it or not. Python has billions of lines of code, so there are countless possibilities to reuse code and learn from carefully constructed examples. Furthermore, the Python community is huge and active, and members are eager to assist newcomers. Since learning Python takes less time than learning many other languages, developers can go right into writing code much sooner; New applications can be created quickly and easily with Python because of how straightforward the language is to use. Python is free, open, and multiplatform; not all languages can make such claims. It is also straightforward to get, install, and deploy.

Learning to code will set one up for success in practically any field, and it's a must if one wants to improve their career in software development or engineering. Python is the most accessible programming language. Knowing Python well opens doors to a wide range of careers and businesses. In the twenty-first century, Python knowledge is power. One will benefit from knowing this even if they never use it at work.

Chapter 1: Introduction to Python

Python is a highly adaptable and extensively utilized high-level programming language renowned for its inherent simplicity and exceptional readability. Python, which was developed by Guido van Rossum and initially made available in 1991, has garnered significant acclaim owing to its simple and concise syntax. Consequently, it has emerged as a highly favourable option for both beginners and proficient programmers. Its design philosophy emphasizes code readability and fewer lines of code, resulting in increased productivity and decreased development time.

1.1 What is Python?

Python's syntax, which is clear, uncluttered, and resembles natural English, makes it so simple. Python employs indentation to define code blocks instead of languages that use complicated symbols and punctuation, making it visually intuitive and lowering the likelihood of syntax errors.

The enhanced readability of Python offers advantages in coding and facilitates collaboration among developers, enabling them to comprehend and sustain Python projects more effortlessly. Python's extensive standard library provides a vast collection of modules and functions to handle a variety of duties, from file manipulation to network communication. This comprehensive library reduces the need to create functionality from scratch, freeing developers to concentrate on more complex issues. Developers may access a sizable ecosystem of specialized tools and frameworks thanks to Python's support for third-party packages through its package management, pip.

Python is adaptable and suitable for a variety of applications. The platform demonstrates proficiency in web development, including frameworks like Django and Flask that streamline the process of constructing websites and web applications. In the field of scientific computing, various libraries like NumPy, SciPy, and pandas offer a range of capabilities that facilitate data manipulation, analysis, and visualization. Libraries such as TensorFlow, PyTorch, and sci-kit-learn provide robust resources for the development and training of models in the fields of machine learning and artificial intelligence.

Additionally, the portability of Python is a significant characteristic. The interpretation of code enables its execution without the requirement of compilation, hence facilitating expedited development and testing processes. This characteristic renders Python well-suited for the purposes of scripting and prototyping. Moreover, Python exhibits platform independence as it is capable of functioning on diverse operating systems such as Windows, macOS, and Linux.

The vitality of Python is enhanced by its community-driven nature. The Python Software Foundation assumes the responsibility of overseeing the development of the Python programming language, thereby ensuring its open-source characteristics and fostering a culture of collaboration among its contributors. The language is enriched by the active participation of the community, which involves the creation of novel libraries, the improvement of pre-existing ones, and the provision of mutual assistance through forums, mailing lists, and online communities.

Nevertheless, it is important to acknowledge that Python does include certain restrictions. The interpretive nature of the language can result in slower execution speeds when compared to compiled languages such as C++ or Java. Although this worry may not be of great significance in many applications, it could potentially pose a challenge in performance-critical jobs. Moreover, the Global Interpreter Lock (GIL) in Python can impose restrictions on its capacity to effectively harness the potential of multi-core processors in the context of multithreaded applications.

1.2 Advantages of Python

- Python's syntax is straightforward and very close to that of the English language, making it a very approachable programming language for novices. It is also a fairly concise language, which means that one can typically write more code in fewer lines than one might with other languages because of how it was designed. Because of this, it is an excellent option for newbies who are just beginning out in the world of computer programming.

- Python is a versatile programming language that can be applied to a wide range of projects, from basic scripting to in-depth data analysis. It is also known for its high level of efficiency. It is also incredibly efficient, making it an excellent choice for situations in which performance is of the utmost importance. Because of this, it is an excellent choice for seasoned developers who are looking for a programming language that is capable of tackling difficult jobs.

- Python is an extremely flexible programming language that can be used for a range of programming paradigms, including object-oriented programming, functional programming, and procedural programming. Python's flexibility makes it a popular choice for software developers. Because of this, it is an excellent option for a diverse range of applications. Python is a general-purpose programming language that may be used for a variety of tasks, including the development of web applications, data science projects, machine learning models, and artificial intelligence systems.

- Python has a huge and active community of developers who contribute to the language and its libraries. This community is responsible for Python's popularity. This indicates that there is a large pool of information at one's disposal to assist them in learning Python and finding solutions to challenges. For instance, there are a lot of online tutorials, books, and forums where one may ask problems and obtain assistance from other people who are developing with Python.

- Python is a programming language that is both free and open source. This means that the language can be used and modified by anybody and that anyone can use it without restriction. Because of this, it is an excellent option for projects in which one will need to be able to communicate their code to other people. Python, for instance, can be used to develop open-source software that anybody can run on their computer and utilize.

1.3 Setting up Python

Python installation on Windows:

Downloading the installer from the official Python website is the first step in installing Python on Windows. Python's most recent version can be found at **https://www.python.org/downloads/windows/**. Double-clicking the installer after downloading it will initiate the installation procedure. Then one will be given instructions on how to complete the installation process, and the installer will ask individuals where they wish to install Python. It is better to leave Python in its default location, C: Python. Click the "Next" button to proceed after selecting a location.

Selecting the components one wants to install is the next step. It is advised to leave the default settings, which include the IDLE programming environment, the Python interpreter, and the documentation. Click the "Next" button to proceed after selecting the components.

The last step is to select the start menu folder where the Python shortcuts will be created. Leave Python 3.8's default folder, as this is what experts advise. After selecting the folder, click "Install" to launch the installation procedure.

After the installation is finished, one should launch the IDLE programming environment by selecting the Python 3.8 folder from the start menu. Thereafter, one can launch the IDLE programming environment, a straightforward text editor that lets one create and execute Python code.

Python installation for Mac:

Downloading the installer from the official Python website is the first step in installing Python on a Mac. Python's most recent version can be found at **https://www.python.org/downloads/mac-osx/.** Double-clicking the installer after downloading it will initiate the installation procedure.

Individuals will be given instructions on how to complete the installation process, and the installer will ask individuals where they wish to install Python. Leave the default location, which is /Library/Python, as it is. After selecting a place, press the "Continue" button to move forward.

Selecting the components one want to install is the next step. Experts advise leaving the default settings, which include the IDLE programming environment, the Python interpreter, and the documentation. Once one has decided on the components, press "Continue" to move further.

To complete the installation, individuals must enter their user password in the final step. After entering the password, select "Install" to launch the installation procedure.

When the installation is finished, click on the Python folder in the Applications folder to launch the IDLE development environment. Thereafter, one can launch the IDLE programming environment, a straightforward text editor that lets one create and execute Python code.

Python installation on Linux:

Opening the terminal is the first step in installing Python on Linux. After starting the terminal, one can install Python by using the apt-get command. Individuals can use the command "apt-get install python3" to install the most recent version of Python.

```
apt-get install python3
```

Individuals will be asked to confirm the installation when they type the command. The installation process will start after they press "y" to confirm.

As an alternative, one can install Python using the package manager for their particular Linux system. For instance, one can run the commands "sudo apt-get install python3" on Ubuntu and "sudo dnf install python3" on Fedora.

```
# for Ubuntu
sudo apt-get install python3

# for Fedora
sudo dnf install python3
```

When the installation is finished, type "python3" in the terminal to launch the Python interpreter. With the Python interpreter now open, one may enter commands and view the results.

```
$ python3

python3>
```

The IDLE development environment, a straightforward text editor that one may use to create and execute Python code, is another option that one has when installing Python. Depending on one's Linux distribution, one can install IDLE with the commands "apt-get install idle3" or "sudo apt-get install idle3."

```
apt-get install idle3
```

PyCharm is another well-liked Python development environment for Linux. Code completion, debugging, and other capabilities are part of this more sophisticated development environment. One can use the installer that is available for download from the official website to set up PyCharm.

1.4 Setting up Python Environment

When setting up a Python environment, an isolated environment is created so that one can install particular Python packages without affecting the system's overall Python installation. To handle dependencies for several projects, this is helpful. Here is how to create a virtual environment to set up a Python environment:

Install Python first:

One should install the most recent version of Python who don't already have it by downloading it from the official Python website (https://www.python.org/downloads/).

Install 'virtualenv':

One can utilize the 'virtualenv' package, which has greater functionality and flexibility, in addition to the built-in'venv' module that Python gives for building virtual environments. Open the

command-line interface (Terminal on Mac/Linux or Command Prompt on Windows) and type the following commands to install it.

```
pip install virtualenv
```

Build a simulated environment:

Select the directory where the virtual environment will be created. Use the command-line interface to get to that directory, then use'venv' (built-in) or 'virtualenv' (third-party) to build a virtual environment:

Using venv (built-in):

```
python -m venv myenv
```

Using virtualenv:

```
virtualenv myenv
```

The name one wants to give their virtual environment should be substituted for "myenv."

Turn on the virtual environment:

Activation commands differ based on one's shell and operating system:

At the Command Prompt on Windows:

```
myenv\Scripts\activate
```

Linux and macOS (Terminal):

```
source myenv/bin/activate
```

One's command-line prompt will alter once it's activated to show in the virtual environment.

Install the packages:

Pip can be used to install Python packages while one's virtual environment is active. For instance:

```
pip install package_name
```

Turn off the virtual environment:

One can deactivate the virtual environment after one has finished using it by using the following command:

```
deactivate
```

Activate the virtual environment once more:

Anytime one wishes to resume working on their project; they can activate the virtual environment once more.

Using the file "requirements.txt":

One can make a "requirements.txt" file that contains a list of all the packages their project depends on in order to manage project dependencies effectively. In one's virtual environment, run the following command to create this file:

```
pip freeze > requirements.txt
```

Use the following instructions to install the prerequisites indicated in the requirements.txt file in a different environment:

```
pip install -r requirements.txt
```

Keep in mind that every project has the option of having its own virtual environment, which guarantees a clear separation of project dependencies. By doing this, conflicts may be avoided and managing the dependencies of one's projects becomes a lot more organized.

Chapter 2: Python Basics

Python's ease of use, readability, and general applicability make it popular among programmers. Starting with Python's basics lays the groundwork for a rewarding journey into the world of coding and problem-solving.

2.1 Python Syntax and Indentation

The concept of indentation in Python is essential, especially considering that incorrect indentation will lead to an IndentationError and prevent the code from being compiled.

Indentation:

Adding white space before a statement in a specific block of code is known as "indentation" in Python. To put it another way, a code block comprises all the statements with the same space to the right.

Example of Python Indentation

If condition (line 2), statement (final line), and statement all belong to the same block, meaning that statement 1 will be run after it. And if the if statement is false, Python will proceed directly to the last sentence to be executed.

The nested if-else structure is part of block 2; thus, if the nested if condition evaluates to False, Python will carry out the instructions inside the corresponding else condition.

The block 3 statements that are contained within nested if-else only execute one statement based on the if-else condition.

Python indentation is a way of formatting code that indicates to the Python interpreter that a collection of statements belongs to a particular block of code. The term "block" refers to any combination of these several statements. A particular purpose may be attributed to the arrangement of statements within a block if one thinks of it in that way. In programming languages such as C, C++, and Java, braces are frequently utilized in the process of defining code blocks. The programming language Python makes use of indentation to emphasize the various sections of code. Indentation is denoted by whitespace when working with Python. All of the statements that have the same amount of whitespace to the right are included within the same block of code. If a block has to be nested further to the left, it is simply given an additional right-hand indentation. One can gain a better understanding of the code by looking at the lines that are presented below.

Code Examples:

Conditional Statements (if, else, elif):

```python
x = 10
if x > 0:
    print("x is positive")
elif x == 0:
    print("x is zero")
else:
    print("x is negative")
```

Loops (for and while):

```python
for i in range(5):
    print(i)

while x > 0:
    print(x)
    x -= 1
```

Function Definitions:

```python
def greet(name):
    print("Hello, " + name)
    print("Welcome to Python!")

greet("Alice")
```

2.2 Variables and Data Types

As the name implies, variables and data types in Python are values that change. A variable in a programming language is a place in memory where one can store a value. The value one has stored might alter in the future in accordance with the requirements. It is formed as soon as a value is assigned to a Python Variable. In Python, declaring a variable does not require any further statements.

One must adhere to specific guidelines when defining variables; to better grasp these guidelines and how to declare variables in Python, let's look at the definition and declaration of variables.

Definition & Declaration of Variable

There are no extra commands in Python for declaring variables. The variable is declared once a value is assigned to it.

```
x = 10
#variable is declared as the value 10 is assigned to it.
```

While declaring a variable, there are a few guidelines to bear in mind:

- The underscore character or a letter must come first in a variable name.

- No number may begin a variable name.

- Only underscores (A-z, 0-9, and _) and alphanumeric characters are permitted in variable names.

- Case matters when naming variables (age, Age, and AGE are all distinct variables).

Data types:

Numerical data types are used in Python to represent and manipulate various types of numbers. Python offers a variety of numerical data types, including:

Integers (int): Whole numbers without a decimal point are known as integers. They could be zero, positive, or negative.

```
x = 5
y = -10
z = 0
```

Floating-Point Numbers (float): Real numbers, including decimal values, are represented using floating-point numbers. The IEEE 754 standard for floating-point arithmetic is used to implement them.

```
a = 3.14
b = -0.5
c = 1.0e-3   # Scientific notation: 0.001
```

Complex Numbers (complex): Real and imaginary parts make up complex numbers. The imaginary portion is denoted by the suffix "j" or "J".

```
comp = 2 + 3j
```

Boolean (bool): 'True' or 'False' are the only two possible truth values that can be represented by the boolean data type. Conditions and logical procedures frequently employ boolean values.

```
is_true = True
is_false = False
```

Other operations on numerical data types supported by Python include arithmetic operations (addition, subtraction, multiplication, division, etc.), comparison operations (greater than, less than, equal to, etc.), and more complex mathematical functions via libraries like "math".

```
# Arithmetic operations
sum_result = 10 + 5
product_result = 3 * 4
quotient_result = 15 / 3

# Comparison operations
is_equal = 7 == 7
is_greater = 10 > 5
is_less_equal = 2 <= 3

# Using math library
import math

sqrt_result = math.sqrt(25)
sin_result = math.sin(math.pi/2)
```

Remember that Python's numerical data types are dynamically typed, so when one assigns a value to a variable, they don't have to explicitly declare the data type. Depending on the value one enters, Python will determine the suitable data type. To ensure correct computations and prevent unexpected code behaviour, it's critical to grasp the traits and constraints of each numerical data type.

2.3 Working with Strings

In Python, strings are among the most widely used types. They are easily made by simply surrounding characters in quotations. Python treats single quotes and double quotes the same way. Assigning a value to a variable and creating a string is really straightforward. For instance,

```
var1 = 'Hello World!'
var2 = "Python Programming"
```

17

Accessing Values in Strings

Python doesn't have a character type; as they are viewed as one-length strings, they are also regarded as substrings.

Substrings can be accessed by using the index or indices to get one's desired substring and the square brackets for slicing. For instance,

```
var1 = 'Hello World!'
var2 = "Python Programming"

print "var1[0]: ", var1[0]
print "var2[1:5]: ", var2[1:5]
```

When the preceding code is executed, the following result is obtained:

```
var1[0]:  H
var2[1:5]:  ytho
```

Updating Strings

By (re)assigning a variable to another string, one can "update" an existing string. The new value may be associated with its prior value or an entirely different string. For instance

```
var1 = 'Hello World!'
print "Updated String :- ", var1[:6] + 'Python'
```

When the preceding code is executed, the following result is produced:

```
Updated String :-  Hello Python
```

Escape Characters

The table below contains a list of escape or non-printable characters that can be represented using backslash notation.

An escape character is interpreted both in single- and double-quoted sequences.

Hexadecimal Character	Backslash Notation	Description
\b	0x08	Backspace
\a	0x07	Bell or alert
\C-x		Control x
\cx		Control x
\e	0x1b	Escape
\v	0x0b	Vertical tab
\s	0x20	Space
\n	0x0a	New line
\t	0x09	Tab
\x		Character x

String Formatting Operator

An interesting feature of Python is the string format operator%. This operator is unique to strings and compensates for the abundance of printf() functions. Here is a basic instance:

```
print "My name is %s and weight is %d kg!" % ('Zara', 21)
```

When the preceding code is executed, the following result is produced:

```
My name is Zara and weight is 21 kg!
```

Here is the complete inventory of symbols that can be used in conjunction with %.

Format Symbol	Conversion
%d	Signed decimal integer
%c	Character
%o	Octal integer

%i	Signed decimal integer
%u	Unsigned decimal integer
%x	Hexadecimal integer (lowercase letters)
%X	Hexadecimal integer (uppercase letters)
%f	Floating point real number
%e	Exponential notation (with lowercase 'e'
%E	Exponential notation (with uppercase 'E'

2.4 Lists, Tuples, and Sets

Python offers a versatile selection of data structures that enable programmers to efficiently manage and manipulate collections of data. Among these structures, lists, tuples, and sets play crucial roles in holding and organizing elements, each with its own distinct characteristics and application scenarios.

Lists: A Dynamic Array for Mutable Sequences

One of the fundamental data structures in Python, lists are renowned for their adaptability and dynamic nature. A list is an ordered compilation of elements separated by commas and enclosed in square brackets [ ]. These elements may be of any data type, including integers, strings, floating-point numbers, and even other lists or complex objects. The distinguishing characteristic of lists is their mutability -- the ability to add, remove, or modify elements after their formation.

The elements of a list can be accessed using zero-based indexing. For example, my_list[0] refers to the list's first item. Additionally, developers can simply extract sublists using slicing. This dynamic indexing enables programmers to efficiently manipulate data, be it a sequence of numbers, a list of names, or a combination of both.

The extensive standard library of Python provides an abundance of list manipulation methods. The append() method adds an item to the end of the list, whereas the insert() method facilitates insertion at a specific index. In contrast, remove() deletes the first instance of a value, whereas

pop() removes and returns the element at a specified index. These functions facilitate the dynamic nature of lists and allow developers to modify lists according to their needs.

Tuples: Immutable Sequences for Data Integrity

Tuples and lists are similar in that they both contain an ordered collection of elements. However, tuples differ in an essential way: they are immutable. While lists can be modified after construction, tuple elements are immutable. This immutability qualifies tuples for use in situations where data integrity and consistency are crucial.

Elements are enclosed in parentheses () to form a tuple. Similar to lists, tuples can contain multiple data types and even additional tuples. Note that attempting to modify a tuple's elements directly will result in an error, even though indexing and slicing function identically to how they do with lists.

In functions that return multiple values, tuples play an important role. Functions can return tuples, enabling developers to store and manipulate multiple data points within a single structure. This function is particularly useful when working with coordinate pairs, date components, or any scenario involving multiple related data points.

Sets: Uniqueness and Set Operations

Sets, a fundamental concept in mathematics, are implemented digitally in Python. A set is an unordered collection of unique elements enclosed by curly braces or constructed with the set() constructor. The uniqueness property enables sets to eliminate duplicate values automatically, making them useful for duties where the distinction is crucial.

Due to their unordered nature, sets do not support indexing, but they excel at membership testing. A straightforward if element in my_set statement efficiently verifies the existence of an element in the set. This property is advantageous for applications such as spelling correction, user authentication, and data deduplication.

In addition to membership testing, sets provide a variety of set operations. The add() method adds a new element to the set, while the remove() method removes a particular element. Among the more complex operations are union (|), intersection (&), and difference (-). These operations enable programmers to compare, combine, and extract elements from sets, making them potent instruments for resolving a variety of problems.

When distinctness and the ability to combine collections are required, sets excel. For example, a developer could use a set to identify unique keywords in a document, ensuring that each keyword is considered only once, while set operations can be used to identify keywords that are shared between two documents.

Choosing the Right Data Structure

The choice between lists, tuples, and sets depends on one's program's specific requirements. For dynamic collections in which elements may alter over time, lists are the method of choice. Tuples are utilized when immutability and data integrity are of the utmost importance. In contrast, sets excel in situations requiring distinct values and efficient membership testing.

Understanding the advantages and disadvantages of these data structures is crucial for writing code that is efficient and maintainable. Lists, tuples, and sets provide a spectrum of tools for manipulating and managing collections of data, each of which is specialized to address specific programming challenges. By selecting the most suitable structure for the task at hand, developers can maximize Python's data manipulation capabilities.

2.5 Dictionaries and Maps

Dictionaries are potent data structures in Python that are used to store and manage collections of data as key-value pairs. A dictionary enables the association of a unique key with a corresponding value, facilitating the efficient and rapid retrieval of data. Due to its mapping character, this data structure is commonly referred to as a "map" in other programming languages.

To construct a dictionary, one should enclose key-value pairs between curly braces and separate them with colons. For instance, my_dict = {'name': 'Alice', 'age': 30} creates a dictionary with two entries: 'name' mapped to 'Alice' and 'age' mapped to 30. Keys must be unique and are typically strings or numbers, whereas values can be of any data type, including integers, strings, lists, and even additional dictionaries.

Dictionary value access is extraordinarily efficient. Using the syntax my_dict[key], one can rapidly retrieve the associated value given a key. This direct access, also known as indexing by key, makes dictionaries ideal for situations where the speed of data retrieval is essential. If a key is not present, accessing it will result in a KeyError. This can be avoided by using the get() method, which returns a default value if the key is not discovered.

Dictionary functionality extends beyond basic retrieval. Adding a new key-value pair is as simple as my_dict['city'] = 'New York', while del my_dict['age'] removes the 'age' entry. Methods such as keys(), values(), and items() enable one to investigate the dictionary's content. It is common to iterate through keys or key-value pairs, particularly when processing large amounts of data.

Dictionaries as Flexible Data Structures

The versatility of dictionaries extends beyond simple data storage. They play a vital role in representing real-world relationships and mapping data in a variety of applications. For instance, a dictionary can contain information about each student in a student database using their roll number as the key. For analysis purposes, sensor data can be associated with timestamps in a scientific experiment.

Nesting dictionaries enable the modelling of more intricate relationships. Hierarchical structures can be formed from dictionaries within dictionaries. This can represent data at multiple granularities. A nested dictionary could, for instance, represent the organizational structure of a corporation, with departments and employees under each department.

Selecting the Appropriate Data Structure

The choice between dictionaries and other data structures is determined by the nature of one's data and the duties one must complete. When data retrieval quickness and mapping relationships are essential, dictionaries excel. When a collection of items must be accessed via a unique identifier, dictionaries offer an effective solution.

When comparing dictionaries with other structures such as lists, tuples, and sets, it is essential to comprehend the characteristics of the data. If one requires duplicated, ordered elements, a list may be preferable. If one needs an organized assortment of unique items, sets are a superior option. Tuples are appropriate when an immutable sequence of constituents is required.

2.6 Basic Input and Output

A programming language's primary objective is to make it interactive with the user and the audience. If one observes closely, the majority of the software one uses in the real world requires user input, whether it's a search engine, an app one uses every day, or even email, where one must first enter their email address and password. In Python, several built-in functions assist in obtaining data from the user and displaying it after applying some logic to the code.

Python Output

Here is displayed some data on the screen using the commonly-used print() statement. One has the option of outputting the information that has been specified on a device (screen) or in a file. Creating statements that clearly output numbers and texts is a requirement of programming in the real world.

Consider an example of how to output a straightforward text.

```
print("Welcome to Python for beginners. In this book, we will learn about Python")
```

For a better comprehension of the syntax of the preceding statement, one has defined the following keywords:

- The values to be presented on the screen are the object(s). They are converted to strings prior to output.

- The sep keyword is used to specify how objects within the same print statement should be separated. By default, sep="indicates a space between two objects.

- The end is used to print a specific value after all values have been printed. By default, the end is n, which creates a new line following each print() statement.

- The file is used to designate where output should be displayed. By default, sys.stdout (the screen) is used.

- The boolean phrase that determines whether False or True is produced is specified by the flush command. The value that is used by default is False. The output that is generated by the print() function in Python is saved in a buffer. When the print() statement is executed, the buffer is cleared out immediately if the flush= True argument is used.

Input and output operations are foundational to every programming language because they enable programs to interact with users and the outside world. In Python, these operations are managed by a variety of built-in functions and libraries, facilitating the efficient exchange of data between programs and their environment.

Input: Collecting User Data

Python provides the 'input()' function to capture command line user input. When 'input()' is invoked, it displays a prompt to the user and waits for them to type a response before the Enter key is pressed. The function returns the user's input as a string that can be saved in a variable or further processed.

```python
user_name = input("Please enter your name: ")
print(f"Hello, {user_name}!")
```

Note that 'input()' returns the user's input as a string; if one anticipates numeric input, one must explicitly convert it using functions such as 'int()' and 'float()'.

Output: Displaying Information

Typically, output in Python is accomplished with the 'print()' function. This function accepts one or more arguments and outputs them to the console as plain text. It is a flexible instrument that can output strings, variables, calculations, and formatted text.

```python
name = "Alice"
age = 30
print("Name:", name)
print("Age:", age)
print(f"{name} is {age} years old.")
```

Input and Output of Files: Reading and Writing Files

Using built-in functions and context managers, Python permits receiving and writing data to and from files. By giving the file's name and the mode in which it should be opened (read, write, etc.), the 'open()' method can be used to open a file. Utilizing the 'with' statement, which generates a context manager and consequently shuts the file when it is no longer required, is strongly suggested for the purpose of ensuring that adequate resource management is carried out.

```python
# Reading from a file
with open("data.txt", "r") as file:
    content = file.read()
    print(content)

# Writing to a file
with open("output.txt", "w") as file:
    file.write("Hello, world!")
```

Python provides modules for sophisticated reading and writing, such as 'csv' for working with comma-separated values and 'json' for working with JSON data. These modules facilitate the management of structured data in various formats.

Formatted Output: Formatting Strings and f-Strings

Python provides numerous output formatting options, which improve readability and presentation. A common method is string formatting, in which the '%' operator is used to replace placeholders with their corresponding values.

```python
name = "Bob"
age = 25
print("Name: %s, Age: %d" % (name, age))
```

In recent versions of Python (3.6 and later), formatting output with f-strings is more concise and intuitive. A string literal is converted into an f-string by prefixing it with the character 'f'. Within an f-string, expressions surrounded by curly braces " are evaluated, and their values are inserted.

```python
name = "Charlie"
age = 40
print(f"Name: {name}, Age: {age}")
```

Input and output operations are required for the development of interactive and useful programs. Python's straightforward input and output functions and libraries facilitate data exchange between programs and users, as well as file viewing and writing. By comprehending these concepts, developers can create applications that are more dynamic, user-friendly, and data-driven.

Chapter 3: Control Flow

There are times in real life when one must make decisions, and based on these choices, one determines what to do next. Similar situations arise in programming where decisions must be made, and the next block of code is executed based on these decisions. In programming languages, decision-making statements determine the flow of program execution (Control Flow).

3.1 Conditional Statements (if, elif, else)

Mastering control flow statements in Python programming is essential for developing dynamic and responsive applications. Control flow enables one to direct the execution of one's code based on certain conditions, thereby making one's programs smarter and more adaptable. Python provides a variety of control flow structures, each of which is suited to particular decision-making scenarios.

If Statement

The if statement is the fundamental decision-making building element in Python. It enables one to determine whether a statement or block of statements should be executed based on the truth or falsity of a condition.

```
if condition:
    # Block of statements to execute if the condition is true
```

In an if statement, the condition evaluates to either true or false. If it evaluates to true, the segment of code that follows it is executed; otherwise, it is skipped.

Python expands upon this fundamental concept by introducing more complex control flow structures.

If-Else Statement

The if-then statement extends the decision-making process beyond a basic binary option. It permits the execution of one segment of code if the condition is true and another if it is false.

```
if condition:
    # Block of statements to execute if the condition is true
else:
    # Block of statements to execute if the condition is false
```

By incorporating an else clause, one allows the program to take alternative actions if the initial condition is not satisfied.

Nested-If Statement

By positioning an if statement within another if statement, nested if statements add complexity. This structure permits the creation of multiple levels of decision-making.

```
if condition1:
    if condition2:
        # Block of statements to execute if both conditions are true
```

If multiple conditions must be met simultaneously for specific actions to be taken, nested if statements are an effective way to achieve this.

If-Elif-Else Ladder

If a single condition must be selected from multiple alternatives, the if-elif-else cascade can help. This structure enables the sequential evaluation of multiple conditions and the execution of the block corresponding to the first true condition.

```
if condition1:
    # Block of statements to execute if condition1 is true
elif condition2:
    # Block of statements to execute if condition2 is true
else:
    # Block of statements to execute if no conditions are true
```

The elif (short for "else if") clauses provide a cascade of alternatives, while the else block functions as a fallback if no conditions are met.

Shorthand If and Ternary Operators

Python provides abbreviated if statements when only one statement is to be executed based on a condition. The abbreviated form simplifies the code by condensing it.

```
statement if condition else alternative_statement
```

This is especially useful when a brief expression will suffice for one's needs.

Real-World Significance

Various scenarios bring control flow structures to life. In a student grading system, for instance, an if-else cascade can classify students based on their grades. Using nested if statements, a shopping application can guide consumers through various product categories based on their preferences. Dynamic and responsive code requires a fundamental understanding and application of control flow statements. By utilizing if statements, if-else structures, nested if statements, if-elif-else ladders, and shorthand forms, Python programmers are able to create logical program flows that are adaptable to shifting conditions and user interactions. This nuanced control over program execution assures the flexibility and adaptability of Python applications in a variety of circumstances.

3.2 Loops (for and while)

Loops are a fundamental component of all programming languages. In a loop structure, a condition is initially evaluated. If this condition is met, some code is executed. The code will continue to execute until the condition becomes invalid.

Consider the pseudo-code section as an example:

```
IF stomach_empty
    eat_food()
ENDIF
//check if stomach is empty again.
IF stomach_empty
    eat_food()
ENDIF
//check if stomach is still empty,
//....
```

Here is a test to see if the stomach_empty variable is true. If this condition is fulfilled, the eat_food method will be executed. Moreover, observe that one's repeatedly entering the same code, which violates the DRY programming principle.

To prevent this issue, one can employ the following loop structure:

```
WHILE stomach_empty //this code will keep on running if stomach_empty is true
    eat_food()
ENDWHILE
```

In this code, a while statement is used. In this case, the loop begins by determining whether the stomach_empty Boolean is true. If this condition is met, the program will continue to execute the eat_food function until it becomes false. In conclusion, developers use loops to repeatedly execute a section of code until a certain condition is met. This results in labour savings and improved code readability.

Types of Loop

There are two types of loop structures in Python:

- for: Repeat a given number of times. This is also referred to as a definite iteration

- while: iterate until the condition is false. This is referred to as an infinite iteration.

For Loop

For iterating over sequences such as lists, tuples, strings, and ranges, the 'for' loop is a workhorse. It simplifies repetitive duties by executing a code block for each sequence element.

```
for element in sequence:
    # Code to be executed for each element
```

During each iteration, 'element' takes on each value from the sequence. This construct is especially useful when iterating through a known set of items, such as a list of names or integers.

For instance:

```
fruits = ["apple", "banana", "cherry"]
for fruit in fruits:
    print(fruit)
```

While Statement

The 'while' loop provides greater flexibility by repeatedly executing a segment of code as long as a specified condition is met. This form of loop is particularly useful when the required number of iterations is unknown.

```
while condition:
    # Code to be executed while the condition is true
```

If the condition does not eventually become false, the cycle will continue forever.

For instance:

```
count = 0
while count < 5:
    print(count)
    count += 1
```

Selecting the Appropriate Loop for the Job

Both 'for' and 'while' loops have their own advantages and are suited to a variety of situations. Use the 'for' loop when iterating over a fixed collection of items and the 'while' loop when the loop should continue as long as a certain condition is met.

Bringing Loops and Control Flow Together

Combining loops with control flow statements, such as 'break' and 'continue', increases their effectiveness. The 'break' statement prematurely departs the loop, whereas the 'continue' statement skips the current iteration and advances to the next.

```
for item in sequence:
    if condition:
        break  # Exit the loop
    if another_condition:
        continue  # Skip this iteration and proceed to the next
    # Code here will execute only if conditions aren't met
```

Loops are fundamental to a wide variety of applications. In a finance application, a 'for' loop can be used to calculate interest for a range of years, whereas a 'while' loop can be used to continue prompting users until they provide valid input. Understanding the 'for' and 'while' loops enables one to automate duties and iterate over data, thereby streamlining and dynamizing code. By incorporating loops into one's programming arsenal, one can efficiently process data, interact with users, and create applications that are responsive and adaptable to various situations. Loops are basic companions on the road to efficient and effective programming, whether one is processing large datasets or navigating users through interactive experiences.

3.3 Break and Continue Statements

The Break Statement:

The "break" statement is a directive that abruptly terminates the loop in which it is located. This interruption is required when a particular condition is met, and further iterations are no longer required.

```
for item in sequence:
    if condition:
        break  # Exit the loop prematurely
    # Other code within the loop
```

In situations where one is seeking a specific value or when a certain threshold has been reached, the "break" statement can save time by terminating the execution of the loop.

For instance:

```
numbers = [2, 4, 6, 8, 10]
for num in numbers:
    if num == 6:
        break  # Stops the loop when num reaches 6
    print(num)
```

The Continue Statement:

The "continue" statement adds a touch of elegance to loops by allowing one to promptly skip the current iteration and proceed to the next. This can be incredibly useful when specific conditions necessitate skipping specific processes.

```
for item in sequence:
    if condition:
        continue  # Skip this iteration and proceed to the next
    # Other code within the loop
```

In a loop, the "continue" statement is frequently used when filtering data or omitting unwanted values.

For instance:

```
numbers = [1, 2, 3, 4, 5, 6, 7, 8, 9, 10]
for num in numbers:
    if num % 2 == 0:
        continue  # Skips even numbers, proceeding to the next iteration
    print(num)
```

3.4 The range () Function

The range() function in Python generates an immutable sequence of numbers from the provided start and stop integers. Range () is a built-in function that returns an object containing a sequence of integers, which can be iterated using a for loop.

Using a for loop with range() in Python, one can repeat an action a given number of times. For instance, let's examine how to use Python 3's range() function to produce the first six integers.

```
# Generate numbers between 0 to 6
for i in range(6):
    print(i)
```

Output:

```
0
1
2
3
4
5
```

3.5 Using Logical Operators

Logical operators in Python are vital tools for making judgments in one's code by evaluating the truth or falsehood of certain situations. Logical operators may be found in the logical package. These operators provide individuals the ability to control the flow of one's program by combining and manipulating boolean values (which can either be True or False). In Python, the most important logical operators are "and," "or," and "not."

And Operator

The "and" operator takes two conditions and determines whether or not both of those circumstances are true before returning True. It will result in False being returned if one of the two conditions are not met. This operator is used rather frequently to check whether or not many requirements are satisfied at the same time.

```
condition1 = True
condition2 = False

result = condition1 and condition2  # Result will be False
```

OR Operator

The "or" operator combines two criteria in the same way as the "and" operator, but it only returns True if at least one of the conditions is accurate. It will only return false if both of the conditions are not met. This operator is helpful for situations in which one want to do an action if any of a number of conditions are satisfied.

```
condition1 = True
condition2 = False

result = condition1 or condition2  # Result will be True
```

NOT Operator:

The "not" operator is a unary operator that can be used in boolean expressions to negate the value of the expression. If the expression evaluates to false, it will return True, and vice versa. This operator is frequently utilized whenever one wishes to invert the results of a condition.

```
condition = True

result = not condition  # Result will be False
```

These logical operators can be coupled to produce circumstances that have a greater degree of complication. In a manner analogous to that of mathematical expressions, parentheses can be utilized to both group expressions and regulate the order in which they are evaluated.

```
condition1 = True
condition2 = False
condition3 = True

result = (condition1 and condition2) or (not condition3)  # Result will be False
```

Logical operators are frequently utilized in control structures such as if statements and loops for the purpose of determining how a program will proceed with its execution in response to a variety of different conditions. The following is an exampleof the use of an if statement:

```
temperature = 25
is_raining = False

if temperature > 30 and not is_raining:
    print("It's a hot and dry day.")
else:
    print("The weather is moderate.")
```

In this example, the computer software determines whether or not the temperature is higher than 30 degrees Celsius and whether or not it is raining. If neither of those conditions are met, it will print a message about a day that is neither hot nor dry; otherwise, it will produce a message about weather that is between the two extremes.

In a nutshell, the logical operators in Python are essential components of the decision-making process in the programming language. The "and" operator combines conditions with the constraint that both conditions must be true. In contrast, the "or" operator needs at least one condition to be true, while the "not" operator modifies the value of a condition in the opposite direction. These operators will assist one in developing adaptable and dynamic programs that can react to a wide variety of scenarios.

Chapter 4: Functions and Modules

Python's built-in functions and modules greatly improve code readability, reusability, and performance. They are essential because of the roles they play in streamlining complicated processes, encouraging modular design, and easing teamwork on programming projects.

4.1 Defining Functions

The Python Functions are a collection of statements that return the desired result. The idea is to group commonly or repeatedly performed tasks into a function so that instead of writing the same code repeatedly for various inputs, one can call the function to reuse the code contained within it.

Some Benefits of Using Functions

* Improve Code Perceivability

* Increase Source code reuse

Python Function Declaration

In Python, functions are essential building blocks that encapsulate a sequence of instructions and can be reused throughout one's program. They contribute to code organization, modularity, and reusability. Python offers two main types of functions: built-in library functions and user-defined functions.

Creating a Function in Python

The 'def' keyword, followed by the function name and a set of parentheses containing the parameters the function will accept, is all that's needed to construct a user-defined function in Python. The code to be run inside the body of a function is written indented below the function's declaration.

```
def fun():
    print("Welcome to GFG")
```

Python Function with Parameters

Python allows one to define functions with parameters, enabling one to pass values to the function when calling it. This is particularly useful when one wants their function to operate on different input data.

```
def add(num1, num2):
    result = num1 + num2
    return result

num1 = 5
num2 = 15
ans = add(num1, num2)
print(f"The addition of {num1} and {num2} results in {ans}.")
```

4.2 Function Arguments and Return Values

Types of Python Function Arguments

Python supports various types of function arguments:

- Default Arguments: These are parameters with default values that are used if no value is provided during the function call.

- Keyword Arguments: These allow one to pass values using parameter names, avoiding the need to remember the order of parameters.

- Positional Arguments: These are arguments passed in the order they are expected by the function.

- Arbitrary Arguments: `args` and `kwargs` are used to pass a variable number of non-keyword and keyword arguments, respectively.

Return Statement in Python Function

The `return` statement is used to exit a function and return a specified value to the caller. It ends the function's execution and can pass back a variable, expression, or constant.

```
def square_value(num):
    """This function returns the square value of the entered number"""
    return num ** 2

print(square_value(2))  # Output: 4
```

Pass by Reference and Pass by Value

In Python, variables are references. When a variable is passed to a function, a new reference to the object is created. Changing the reference inside the function doesn't affect the original reference. However, if the object itself is modified inside the function, the changes are reflected outside the function as well.

```
def modify_list(lst):
    lst.append(5)

my_list = [1, 2, 3, 4]
modify_list(my_list)
print(my_list)  # Output: [1, 2, 3, 4, 5]
```

4.3 Lambda Functions

Lambda functions, also known as anonymous functions, are compact and versatile tools in Python that allow one to create small, inline functions on the fly. These functions are particularly useful for situations where one needs a simple function without the overhead of defining a full-fledged named function.

Basic Syntax of Lambda Functions

The syntax of a lambda function is straightforward:

lambda arguments: expression

Any number of arguments may be passed to a lambda function, but only one expression may be present. The result of the expression is the value returned by the lambda function

Utilizing and Developing Lambda Functions

Lambda functions are frequently used when a comprehensive function definition would be excessive for a brief operation. In situations where one need a quick function for a specific operation, such as sorting or filtering data, they are excellent.

```
# A lambda function to square a number
square = lambda x: x * x

print(square(5))  # Output: 25

# Using lambda function for sorting
points = [(1, 2), (3, 1), (0, 4)]
points_sorted = sorted(points, key=lambda point: point[1])

print(points_sorted)  # Output: [(3, 1), (1, 2), (0, 4)]
```

The Advantages of Lambda Functions

- Lambda functions allow one to write code that is concise by expressing basic operations concisely.

- When the operation is brief and self-explanatory, using a lambda function can improve the readability of the code by eliminating the need for ancillary named functions.

- Singular use Lambda functions are ideal for tiny, one-time operations where a named, dedicated function is not required.

Lambda Function Limitations

Lambda functions have their role, but they are not appropriate for all circumstances. They cannot contain multiple statements or complex logic and are limited to basic expressions. For more complex operations, a complete function definition is recommended.

4.4 Modules and Importing

In the realm of programming, as projects grow and complexity increases, the need for code organization and reusability becomes paramount. Python modules and the concept of importing allow one to structure their code into manageable units and incorporate external functionality seamlessly.

Understanding Python Modules

A module in Python is a file containing Python definitions, statements, and functions. It serves as a container for related code, helping one organize, reuse, and modularize their program. Python's standard library provides a plethora of modules that cover a wide range of functionalities.

Creating One's Own Module

To create one's own module, simply save the code in a **.py** file with a meaningful name. This file will become one's module, and one can import and use its contents in other scripts.

For example, if one has a file named **math_operations.py** containing mathematical functions:

```
# math_operations.py

def add(x, y):
    return x + y

def subtract(x, y):
    return x - y
```

Importing Modules

Once one has created the module, one can import it into other Python scripts using the **import** statement. This allows one to access the functions and variables defined in the module.

```
# main_script.py

import math_operations

result = math_operations.add(5, 3)
print(result)  # Output: 8
```

Importing Specific Functions or Variables

One can also import specific functions or variables from a module using the **from** keyword.

```
# main_script.py

from math_operations import add

result = add(5, 3)
print(result)  # Output: 8
```

Using Aliases

To make one's code more readable or to avoid naming conflicts, one can import modules or functions using aliases.

```
# main_script.py

import math_operations as math_ops

result = math_ops.add(5, 3)
print(result)  # Output: 8
```

Exploring Python's Standard Library

Python's standard library is a treasure trove of pre-built modules that offer a wide range of functionalities. Modules for file manipulation, regular expressions, networking, and more are readily available for use.

Third-party Modules and Packages

For extended functionality beyond the standard library, Python's package ecosystem provides thousands of third-party modules. These can be installed using tools like **pip** and integrated into one's code.

4.5 Standard Library Overview

Python's standard library is a vast collection of pre-built modules and packages that offer a vast array of functionalities, making it an indispensable resource for developers. From working with files and data to networking and regular expressions, the standard library provides a variety of programming tools.

File Manipulation and Control

The 'os' module enables file operations, directory manipulation, and path management by facilitating interaction with the operating system.

```python
import os

# Check if a file exists
if os.path.exists("myfile.txt"):
    print("File exists")
else:
    print("File does not exist")
```

Serialization and Persistence of Data

The 'pickle' module of Python enables the serialization of Python objects into a file-saveable format, making it useful for data persistence.

```python
import pickle

data = {'name': 'Alice', 'age': 30}
with open('data.pkl', 'wb') as f:
    pickle.dump(data, f)
```

Regular Expressions

There's module provides tools for working with regular expressions, permitting string manipulation and pattern matching.

```python
import re

text = "Hello, my email is alice@example.com"
pattern = r'\w+@\w+\.\w+'
email = re.search(pattern, text).group()
print(email)
```

Connectivity and Internet Access

The 'urllib' module enables retrieval of data from URLs, HTTP requests, and web content processing.

```python
import urllib.request

response = urllib.request.urlopen("https://www.example.com")
html = response.read().decode('utf-8')
print(html)
```

Date and Hour

The 'datetime' module facilitates operations such as formatting and time zone conversions by allowing manipulation of dates and times.

```
from datetime import datetime

now = datetime.now()
print("Current date and time:", now)
```

Data Processing

The 'csv' module provides utilities for reading and writing CSV files, which makes data manipulation and processing seamless.

'''For example: '''python import csv'''

```
with open('data.csv', 'r') as file:
    reader = csv.reader(file)
    for row in reader:
        print(row)
```

Mathematical and Statistical Studies

The 'math' module provides numerous mathematical functions, such as trigonometry and logarithms.

```
import math

x = math.sqrt(25)
print(x)  # Output: 5.0
```

Chapter 5: Object-Oriented Programming (OOP)

Object-oriented programming (OOP) is a strong programming paradigm that centres on organizing code in relation to "objects," which are concrete representations of abstract classes. In order to improve code readability, maintainability, and scalability, OOP advocates organizing code into reusable and modular components. Let's dive into Python's Object-Oriented Programming and its core concepts.

5.1 Introduction to OOP

Object-oriented programming, commonly referred to as OOP, is a technique for organizing the components of a computer program into distinct objects that share similar characteristics and actions. One will become familiar with the fundamentals of object-oriented programming in Python by following along with the material below.

In a conceptual sense, objects can be compared to the parts that make up a system. Imagine a program to be somewhat like an assembly line in a factory. The raw materials are processed by a component of the system at each stage of the assembly line, which finally results in the transformation of the raw materials into the finished product

Object-oriented programming is a paradigm of programming that offers a means of organising programs in such a way that their characteristics and behaviours are bundled into separate objects. This is accomplished through the use of an object-oriented programming language.

For example, an item may stand in for a person by having attributes like a name, age, and address, as well as actions like walking, talking, breathing, and running. Or, it might be a representation of an email containing characteristics such as a recipient list, topic, and body, as well as activities such as attaching files and sending them.

Object-oriented programming is a technique for simulating interactions between virtual entities, such as a car, and real-world entities, such as a company and its employees. Object-oriented programming may also be thought of as a strategy for modelling abstract concepts like companies. OOP represents the elements of the actual world as software objects, each of which is assigned some data and is able to carry out a set of predefined operations.

In procedural programming, a program is structured like a cookbook, with a series of stages laid down in a linear fashion in the form of functions and code blocks. Another typical programming paradigm is this one.

Not only do objects in object-oriented programming in Python represent the data, as they do in procedural programming, but they also play a role in the overall structure of the program. This is the most important lesson from object-oriented programming in Python. Data, such as the raw or preprocessed materials present at each stage on an assembly line, and behaviour, such as the action carried out by each component of the assembly line, are both components of an object.

5.2 Classes and Objects

Define a Class in the Python Language

Primitive data structures, such as numbers, strings, and lists, are intended to represent elementary bits of data, such as the price of an apple, the title of a poem, or one's preferred colour palette, respectively. What should one do if they want to portray something that is more complicated?

Take, for instance, the case when one needs to keep tabs on the workers in an organization. One must keep a record of some fundamental information regarding each employee, such as their name, age, position, and the year they began working for the company.

One way to accomplish this is to present each employee in the form of a list as follows:

```
kirk = ["James Kirk", 34, "Captain", 2265]
spock = ["Spock", 35, "Science Officer", 2254]
mccoy = ["Leonard McCoy", "Chief Medical Officer", 2266]
```

This strategy is fraught with difficulties on account of a variety of factors.

To begin, managing larger code files can become more challenging as a result of this. Will should remember that the element with index 0 is the employee's name even if they make a reference to kirk[0] on a line that is several lines away from the line where the kirk list is declared?

Second, it raises the possibility of errors occurring because not every employee will have the same number of items on the list. The age is not included in the McCoy list that is shown above, which is why mccoy[1] will return "Chief Medical Officer" rather than Dr McCoy's actual age.

Using classes is a fantastic technique to make this kind of code more comprehensible and easier to maintain than it would otherwise be.

Compared to Instances

Classes are what is utilized in the process of constructing user-defined data structures. Classes provide behaviours and actions that an object produced from the class can conduct with its data. These behaviours and actions are referred to as methods, and classes call these functions.

Here individuals are going to learn how to create a class called Dog in this tutorial. This class will store some information about the qualities and behaviours that a specific dog may have.

A class is a sort of template that specifies how something ought to be defined. In reality, it does not include any data at all. The Dog class mandates that a dog be given a name and an age in order to be defined, but the class itself does not include the name or age of any particular dog.

An object built from a class containing actual data is referred to as an instance. The class serves as the blueprint for the object. There is no longer a blueprint that represents an instance of the Dog class. It's a real dog, and he has a name like Miles. He's four years old now.

To put it another way, a class can be compared to a questionnaire or form. An instance is analogous to a form that has been finished and submitted by entering data. Multiple instances can be derived from a single class in the same way that a single form can be completed by multiple individuals, each with its own specific information.

A Guide to the Definition of a Class

Every single class definition must begin with the class keyword, which is then followed by the class's actual name and a colon. It is regarded to be a part of the class's body, any piece of code that is indented below the class definition.

The following is an example of a dog class:

```
class Dog:
    pass
```

One statement—specifically, the pass keyword—makes up the entirety of the Dog class's implementation. Pass is frequently employed in programming as a stand-in for the location where the code will ultimately go. It enables one to run this code without causing an error to be generated by Python.

Let's make the Dog class a little more interesting by defining certain properties that are required for all Dog objects. The Dog class isn't particularly intriguing right now, so let's make it that way. Name, age, coat colour, and breed are just some of the determinants that are up for grabs on one end of the bargaining table. Just one's name and age will do; if one wants to keep things as straightforward as possible.

A method with the name.__init__() is responsible for the definition of the properties that all Dog objects must possess. The.__init__() function is called whenever a new Dog object is created. This function is responsible for setting the initial state of the object by assigning values to the Dog object's properties. In other words, the.__init__() function is responsible for initializing each new instance of the class.

One can pass.__init__() any number of parameters, but the first one will always be a variable called self. One can pass any number of parameters to.__init__(). When a new instance of a class is formed, that instance is immediately sent to the self parameter of the.__init__() function. This allows additional attributes to be defined on the object that the class represents.

Let's make some changes to the Dog class by adding a new __init__() method that generates the.name and.age attributes:

```
class Dog:
def __init__(self, name, age):
    self.name = name
    self.age = age
```

Please take note that the signature of the.__init__() method has been indented by four spaces. There are eight spaces before the body of the procedure that is being described. The indentation in question is of the utmost significance. It explains to Python that the.__init__() method should be considered a part of the Dog class.

There are two statements that use the self variable within the body of the.__init__() function. They are as follows:

When one uses the formula self.name = name, an attribute called name is created, and the value of the name parameter is assigned to it.

The expression self.age = age produces an attribute with the name age and gives it the value specified by the age input.

Instance attributes are the attributes that are produced in the.__init__() function. The value of an instance attribute is unique to the particular instance of a class that it is associated with. There is a name and an age associated with every Dog object, but the specific values of the name and age attributes will change depending on the specific Dog instance.

Class attributes, on the other hand, are qualities that are constant across all instances of a class and have the same value. Outside of the.__init__() function, one can define a class attribute by giving a value to a variable name that has already been declared.

The following Dog class, for instance, contains a class attribute named species, and it has the value "Canis familiaris":

```
    class Dog:
# Class attribute
species = "Canis familiaris"

def __init__(self, name, age):
    self.name = name
    self.age = age
```

The definitions of class attributes are placed just beneath the line that contains the class name on the first line of the declaration, and they are indented by four spaces. They are required to have an initial value assigned to them at all times. When an instance of the class is created, the class's attributes are also automatically created and given their initial values at the same time.

Define the properties of a class using its attributes if one wants each instance of the class to have the same value for those properties. When working with properties that differ from one instance to the next, instance attributes should be used.

5.3 Constructors and Destructors

Constructors

A constructor is a particular method contained within a class that generates and initialises an instance of that class. Constructors are also known as "initialization methods." Constructors can be broken down into a few distinct categories. When an instance of a class is created, the corresponding constructor is called upon involuntarily.

A constructor is a one-of-a-kind function that gets called whenever an object of a particular class is created. This happens automatically. The primary function of a constructor is to either populate the data members of a class with default values or add new values to those members. It is not possible for it to return any value other than zero.

Syntax of Python Constructor

```
def __init__(self):
    # initializations
```

The __init__ function is a reserved function (sometimes known as a dunner method) in Python. Constructor is the term used for this component in Object-Oriented Programming.

Different Categories of Constructors

There are two distinct kinds of constructors in Python, and they are as follows:

• Parameterized Constructor

• Default Constructor

Parameterized Constructor

The term "parameterized constructor" refers to a constructor that, in addition to accepting "self," also accepts arguments.

Within the confines of the class, these parameters may be put to use in order to assign values to the data members. As an example:

```
class Details:
    def __init__(self, animal, group):
        self.animal = animal
        self.group = group

obj1 = Details("Crab", "Crustaceans")
print(obj1.animal, "belongs to the", obj1.group, "group.")
```

As a result:

```
Crab belongs to the Crustaceans group.
```

Default Constructer

A constructor is referred to as having Default behaviour when it does not take any parameters from the object being constructed and only takes one argument in the form of self within the constructor. As an example:

```
class Details:
  def __init__(self):
    print("animal Crab belongs to Crustaceans group")
obj1=Details()
```

As a result:

```
animal Crab belongs to Crustaceans group
```

Decorator

One is able to change the behaviour of functions and methods by using a tool called a Python decorator, which is a powerful and adaptable piece of software. They allow the functionality of a function or method to be expanded without requiring the underlying source code to be modified.

A function known as a decorator is one that modifies the behaviour of another function by passing it as an argument to itself and returning a new function with the modified behaviour of the first function. This new function is what's known as a "decorated" function, and it's been around for a while. The following is an example of the fundamental syntax required to use a decorator:

```
@decorator_function
def my_function():
    pass
```

The following piece of code can be written using the @decorator_function notation as a shortcut.

```
def my_function():
    pass
my_function = decorator_function(my_function)
```

Decorators are frequently used to add new functionality to existing methods and functions. Some examples of this functionality include logging, memoization, and access control.

Example of a Use-Case Scenario

The addition of logging is a popular application of decorators, which is one of their many uses. For instance, one can use a decorator in order to record the parameters that are passed to a function as well as the result that it returns after each time that function is called:

```python
import logging

def log_function_call(func):
    def decorated(*args, **kwargs):
        logging.info(f"Calling {func.__name__} with args={args}, kwargs={kwargs}")
        result = func(*args, **kwargs)
        logging.info(f"{func.__name__} returned {result}")
        return result
    return decorated

@log_function_call
def my_function(a, b):
    return a + b
```

This demonstration shows how the log_function_call decorator works by taking a function as an input and returning a new function that logs the function call both before and after the original function is run.

Decorators are a feature in Python that may be used to add functionality to functions and methods without having to edit the source code for those functions and methods. Decorators are a strong and flexible feature in Python. They are an excellent tool for separating concerns, cutting down on code duplication, and making one's code easier to read and keep up to date. Decorators in Python are a technique to extend the usefulness of functions and methods by adjusting their behaviour without modifying the source code. This is accomplished by decorating the functions and methods with additional data. They are put to use for a wide range of tasks, including logging, memorization, access control, and a great deal more besides. It is a powerful tool that may be used to make one's code more readable, maintainable, and expandable. One can use it in a number of different ways.

5.4 Inheritance and Polymorphism

Inheritance and polymorphism are two significant ideas that Python offers within the field of Object-Oriented Programming (OOP), both of which contribute to the organization, reusability, and adaptability of program code. These ideas are crucial to the process of developing well-structured and effective software. They enable programmers to build upon previously written code

and make it possible for a wide variety of objects to interact with one another in a smooth manner. Building on top of preexisting structures is one example of inheritance.

Inheritance is a fundamental concept in Object-Oriented Programming (OOP) that permits the creation of new classes that are descended from existing classes, also known as base or parent classes. These descended classes are referred to as derived or child classes. A hierarchical relationship can be established between classes by the use of this method, which enables child classes to inherit the traits and behaviours of their parents' classes. Reusing code is made easier through inheritance, which also helps cut down on unnecessary repetition and makes it simpler to develop new capabilities.

Imagine one is in charge of developing a management system for a zoo, One can develop a base class called "Animal" that incorporates these shared characteristics rather than designing individual classes for each animal's typical actions, such as eating and sleeping, which are examples of common behaviours. After that, one can derive individual animal classes from the basic class, such as "Lion" and "Elephant," which will inherit the traits of the base class while also adding their own unique characteristics.

```python
class Animal:
    def eat(self):
        print("Animal is eating.")

class Lion(Animal):
    def roar(self):
        print("Roar!")

class Elephant(Animal):
    def trumpet(self):
        print("Trumpet!")
```

Python class Animal has a function called eat(self), which prints out the message.

In this demonstration, the "eat" method is inherited by both the "Lion" and "Elephant" classes because it is inherited from the "Animal" base class. This inheritance encourages a modular approach to programming, which centralizes commonly used properties and behaviours in order to reduce the amount of redundant code that must be written.

Polymorphism is defined as the ability to change appearance while maintaining functionality. In object-oriented programming (OOP), polymorphism is a fundamental idea that encourages flexibility and extensibility. It makes it possible for objects from various classes to be regarded as if they were instances of the same superclass. This makes it possible for these objects to be used interchangeably. This idea is summed up perfectly in the term "one interface, many implementations."

Take into consideration the possibility that someone is developing a drawing application that has several different form classes, such as circle, square, and triangle. Polymorphism enables them to communicate with all shapes through a shared interface, despite the fact that each shape has its own drawing implementation that is specific to it.

```python
class Shape:
    def draw(self):
        pass

class Circle(Shape):
    def draw(self):
        print("Drawing a circle.")

class Square(Shape):
    def draw(self):
        print("Drawing a square.")

class Triangle(Shape):
    def draw(self):
        print("Drawing a triangle.")
```

Because of polymorphism, it is possible to iterate over a list of shapes and call the draw method for each shape individually, notwithstanding the unique class each shape belongs to. This simplifies the code and makes it easier to maintain while simultaneously promoting a standard method for interacting with a wide variety of objects.

The Advantages and the Importance of It

Both inheritance and polymorphism offer a number of benefits that help make software development more effective and easier to maintain, including the following:

- Code Reusability: Inheritance gives one the ability to reuse previously written code, which helps to reduce instances of repetition and advances the "Don't Repeat Yourself" (DRY) philosophy.

- Modular Design: Modular development is made easier by inheritance and polymorphism, which enables teams to work on individual components without depending on the efforts of other teams.

- Hierarchical Structure: Inheritance helps to construct a clear hierarchy among classes, which better reflects the relationships that exist in the actual world and makes it easier to organize code.

- Customization and Extension: Derived classes have the ability to change the properties and behaviours they acquire in order to conform to specific requirements. This helps stimulate customization.

- Polymorphism ensures consistent interaction with objects through common interfaces, enhancing the code's predictability.

- Scalability and future-proofing: Polymorphism makes it possible to integrate new classes into an application while maintaining compatibility with its existing interfaces. This makes polymorphism an important feature for ensuring future scalability.

In Python, the concepts of inheritance and polymorphism are powerful tools that enable programmers to construct software that is well-organized, flexible, and easy to maintain. These ideas promote effective cooperation, code reusability, and interface standardization by expanding upon pre-existing computer programs and by developing shared protocols. The examples of a zoo management system and a drawing application demonstrate how these ideas can be used to simplify difficult circumstances. This enables developers to concentrate on high-level design while also ensuring that their code is cohesive and extensible. One will be able to design agile software that is adaptable to changing requirements and that will stand the test of time if one accepts inheritance and polymorphism and then harness the full power of object-oriented programming (OOP).

5.5 Encapsulation and Abstraction

Every programmer strives to build a tidy and clean code, and to do so, he needs to utilize an appropriate weapon, such as OOP ideas or armour. When suitable OOP ideas are used, the complexity of the code will be reduced, and the entity of the objects will be detached from other sections of the code. Additionally, it makes the text easier to read and can be readily updated if necessary.

In addition, OOP concepts such as inheritance make it possible to write code that is extensible. These ideas come in handy when establishing abstract classes, altering programs that have already been put into place, and putting together an application for use in real-world situations.

Abstraction

Abstraction refers to the technique of concealing irrelevant data while revealing only the necessary facts. One is just keeping the transparency of a small portion of the data available to the customer

out of an ocean's worth of data. This fundamental idea of object-oriented programming will make the code easier to read and simpler while at the same time reducing its overall complexity.

For instance, suppose that one has been tasked with developing a portal for online course enrollment and that the data fields that are available include the following: sibling's name, college name, age, course name, current occupation, payment method, marital status, name, and car number.

After having a look at the data fields that are available, individuals will come to the realization that some of the information is not required for the course registration portal. Fields such as "sibling's name," "marital status," and "vehicle number" are examples of fields that are not required for course enrollment.

Therefore, one needs to be specific and select only the data that is pertinent. Now the required fields are "name, age, current occupation, college name, course name, payment method," and this constitutes an example of abstraction in object-oriented programming (OOP) due to the fact that individuals have escorted selected information from the entire data set.

This new data can now also be utilized for certain other applications, such as a tracker for the current status of the course, a record of the course's completion, and so on. Aone can be able to use the same data without making any modifications.

The concepts of abstraction and abstract class are commonly misconstrued by individuals. Are there any connections between the two?

Abstraction should not be confused with an abstract class. Abstract classes and methods are developed with the goal of having a child class or subclass eventually implement their functionality. At the same time, abstraction consists of only concealing the data and displaying only the data that is pertinent through the utilization of access specifiers such as public, protected, and private.

One needs to have a solid understanding of the concept behind both Encapsulation and Abstraction before one can move on to discussing the differences between the two. The ability to cope with complicated abstractions is made possible through hierarchical classification. In addition to this, it assists one in designing layered semantics as well as breaking down complicated systems into more manageable parts. As a result, abstraction places its primary emphasis on generalizing components that are essential to the system design process. In other words, it concentrates only on the most significant aspects.

Encapsulation

The process of connecting the data members with the member variables is known as encapsulation. Because of this, direct access to variables won't be necessary, which is good news because direct access to variables can compromise users' privacy, and hiding the implementation won't be an option.

The amount of one's code that is displayed to the user is cut down significantly by encapsulation. Anyone who uses their code after it has been published or any part of their code after it has been published might be considered a user.

Encapsulation functions much like a protective wrapper, concealing both the data and the code that are contained within a class. That data and code will be accessed externally, outside of the method/member function, as well as the class which does not belong to that class's members.

In class, readers may have covered some traditional methods like set and get. The set method is used to modify or allot a value to a variable, while the get method is used to read or retrieve the value of a variable. Both of these techniques are considered to be programming fundamentals. Here, one is able to immediately access the variables by using the object of that class; however, if one wants to keep a variable private, one will need to make use of the settings and get methods.

The idea is straightforward: all that needs to be done is to make the get and set methods public while keeping the variables private. Since private objects are inaccessible outside of the class but are available for use within the class, the only way to access the variables is by using the public methods that are available outside of the class. Encapsulation refers to the process of attaching variables to methods or otherwise grouping them together.

Advantages of Abstraction

- Since the user can only see the data that is relevant to them, the privacy of the data may be maintained.

- Streamlines the complexity of the code while simultaneously improving its readability. It is possible to utilize the class that implements the abstraction as a parent class by inheriting its capabilities; this improves reusability and reduces the amount of duplication in the code.

- The ability to extend functionality and reduce the complexity of reworking are two benefits of abstraction.

- When working at a higher degree of abstraction, one should focus more on communicating about the behaviour and less on communicating about the technology.

- It permits an accurate simulation of a situation that could occur in the actual world. It encourages creative problem-solving, which may be put to use in the actual world.

- Because new objects may be developed with only little variations from the current ones, it makes it much easier to maintain and modify the code that is already in place.

- It provides a good structure for code libraries, within which the programmer has the ability to readily customize the software components that are given. Its primary value lies in its contribution to GUI development.

- When one makes changes to their code that are implemented with an abstraction, the users of the abstraction do not need to make changes to their code. Users are only required to modify their code in the event that the abstraction is altered.

- When writing code that makes use of abstraction, the code that is written can be reused against any new code that executes the abstraction. As a result, one is able to accomplish more with less coding.

- The choice can then be reflected in a different section of the original code thanks to the use of extension points, which are utilized by abstraction. This decision could be made in any area of the program, in another program, or during runtime. All three options are possible.

Advantages of Encapsulation.

- It provides assistance in the process of binding the data members with the member functions.

- Enhances both the effectiveness and the friendliness of the user interface for error analysis.

- The programmer is given a great deal of leeway in terms of controlling the data's accessibility and openness because of this feature.

- The user of the code does not rely on the component of the program that is forecasted to undergo changes. When one makes changes to their application, the users do not need to make changes to their code.

- One has effective control over the way in which one's program's code and state evolve throughout the course of its lifespan. When something is encapsulated, it ensures that there will be fewer unforeseen problems that need to be fixed.

What Is the Difference Between Encapsulation and Abstraction?

Definition:

Hiding the specifics of how the code is implemented and written is what abstraction is. To encapsulate anything means to conceal its data while also restricting who can see its code.

Phase:

The process of abstraction occurs at the design level. The process of encapsulation occurs at the implementation level.

Pivotal Ability:

Instead of being concerned with how a class is implemented, abstraction concentrates on the capabilities of individual class instances. Encapsulation lends a hand in data binding and gives users more flexibility over how transparent their data is kept.

Use Case:

At the stage of developing a project, reducing the complexity is one of the primary goals of the abstraction process, which is a design-level process. At the implementation stage of a project, encapsulation is a procedure that is used to ensure privacy and preserve control over the openness of data. This is done through the use of a method known as implementation-level encapsulation.

How to Implement:

In Python, abstraction can be accomplished through the use of classes and interfaces. Classes can also be used to implement encapsulation, and control over the data's privacy can be acquired by setting access specifiers such as protected, public, and private. Encapsulation can also be used in this way.

Focus:

The focal point is where one finds the most significant distinction between encapsulation and abstraction. Encapsulation places more of an emphasis on the processes that need to be followed, whereas abstraction is more concerned with the tasks themselves. If one wants to build solutions more quickly in Python, one will find it helpful to have a firm grasp of the distinction between abstraction and encapsulation. As an example:

An example can help one comprehend the difference between encapsulation and abstraction. The graphical user interfaces of mobile phones make advantage of abstraction. When one clicks on the icons, abstraction enables them to carry out the functions that are associated with them. Let's look at an example of encapsulation to better understand the difference between encapsulation and abstraction. When the user clicks on the icon, the encapsulation process begins in the background to direct the user through the subsequent steps.

Data representation:

The manner in which data is represented is one of the key ways in which Java's Abstraction and Encapsulation differ significantly from one another. Encapsulation encloses both the data and the codes for essential information, whereas abstraction just reflects the data that is valuable. In addition to that, it makes it easier for engineers to organize the entire code.

Hiding:

A more abstract viewpoint is provided by abstraction, which, in turn, conceals the complexity of the situation. The inner workings of the system are hidden through encapsulation, which makes it easier to make changes in the future.

Program partition:

The manner in which Java applications are partitioned represents yet another significant distinction between Encapsulation and Abstraction. The software can be broken up into a number of discrete pieces using abstraction, whereas using encapsulation makes it simple to modify the code to meet the program's evolving needs.

Problem-solving:

On the design level, problems are solved by abstraction, whereas on the implementation level, problems are solved through encapsulation.

Abstraction and Encapsulation

The distinctions between Java's Abstraction and Encapsulation are not restricted solely to the aforementioned categories and features. In order to have a complete understanding of the distinction between abstraction and encapsulation in Python, one must also be familiar with the strategies that are used to address issues that arise in the real world. An example of abstraction from the real world:

To begin, here is an example of a banking application to better comprehend the difference between encapsulation and abstraction. Imagine someone is tasked with developing a banking application and told to compile a list of all the information they know about one's client. During the process of designing a banking application, they can collect some details that are not useful. As a result, they will need to select only the most pertinent information, such as one's name, address, and other financial details. Abstraction is the process of retrieving, eliminating, and selecting consumer information from a large pool of data. Once the information has been recovered, it can be put to use in a variety of different applications. For instance, one needs just make a few minor adjustments to the data before using it to apply for jobs on job portals, apply for jobs in hospitals, apply for jobs in government databases, etc. As a result, one can utilize it as one's Master Data.

Chapter 6: File Handling

When it comes to storing and retrieving data, files are an absolute necessity in the world of programming. Python provides its users with a complete range of tools and functions to facilitate the efficient management of files. In this chapter, readers will delve into the world of file handling in Python, investigating how to read from and write to files, handle various file formats, and manage exceptions related to file operations. Specifically, individuals will look at how to read from and write to files in Python.

6.1 Opening and Closing Files

Open and shut file operations are handled by built-in methods in Python. When one is through working with a file, they can close it using the 'close()' method, which was previously referred to as the 'open()' function.

```python
# Opening a file in read mode
file_path = "example.txt"
file = open(file_path, "r")  # 'r' for read mode

# Perform operations on the file
content = file.read()
print(content)

# Closing the file
file.close()
```

It is imperative to close files after utilizing them so that system resources can be made available. Nevertheless, if one wants to take a more secure and up-to-date method, one can use the 'with' statement, which handles file closure automatically:

```python
with open(file_path, "r") as file:
    content = file.read()
    print(content)
# File is automatically closed when the block is exited
```

6.2 Reading from Files

Python provides a variety of techniques to read data from files, including the following:

Reading the Entire File

When one uses the read ()' method, they are able to read the entirety of the contents of a file. The contents of the file are read into a string using this function.

```
with open("example.txt", "r") as file:
    content = file.read()
    print(content)
```

Reading Line by Line

Reading larger files line by line is frequently the more time-effective method to use. In order to accomplish this, one can make use of the deadline ()' method.

```
with open("example.txt", "r") as file:
    line = file.readline()
    while line:
        print(line, end="")
        line = file.readline()
```

Reading All Lines into a List

The'readlines()' method allows one to read all of the lines from a file into a list for further processing.

```
with open("example.txt", "r") as file:
    lines = file.readlines()
    for line in lines:
        print(line, end="")
```

6.3 Writing to Files

It is just as vital to write data to files as it is to read them. Python offers a number of different options for writing to files:

Writing to an Empty File

Using the 'write()' method, one can either create a new file or overwrite an existing file with its contents.

```
with open("new_file.txt", "w") as file:
    file.write("Hello, world!\n")
    file.write("This is a new file.")
```
Appen

ding to a File

Use the 'a' (append) mode when one wishes to add material to an existing file without overwriting the one that is there already.

```
with open("existing_file.txt", "a") as file:
    file.write("This content will be appended.")
```

6.4 Handling File Exceptions

It is essential, while working with files, to handle any potential exceptions that can occur, such as when a file cannot be located or when there is a problem with permissions.

```
try:
    with open("nonexistent_file.txt", "r") as file:
        content = file.read()
        print(content)
except FileNotFoundError:
    print("File not found.")
except PermissionError:
    print("Permission denied.")
except Exception as e:
    print("An error occurred:", str(e))
```

6.5 Closing Thoughts

Handling files is a key skill in programming because it enables one to interface with data sources that are external to one's application. Whether one is reading, writing, or adding data to a file, working with files in Python is a breeze because of the programming language's in-built functions and user-friendly syntax. By gaining knowledge of these principles and putting them into practice, one will acquire the ability to manage numerous file operations in one's Python applications in an efficient manner.

6.6 Working with Various Formats of Files

In addition to plain text, Python supports a variety of other file formats. Consider the following examples of common situations:

Reading and writing CSV files is covered in this section.

It is usual practice to store tabular data in a format known as CSV, which stands for comma-separated values. Reading and writing CSV files are made much easier in Python with the 'csv' package.

```python
import csv

# Reading a CSV file
with open("data.csv", "r") as csv_file:
    csv_reader = csv.reader(csv_file)
    for row in csv_reader:
        print(row)

# Writing to a CSV file
data = [
    ["Name", "Age"],
    ["Alice", 25],
    ["Bob", 30],
]
with open("new_data.csv", "w", newline="") as csv_file:
    csv_writer = csv.writer(csv_file)
    csv_writer.writerows(data)
```

Reading and writing JSON files is covered in this section.

Interchanging structured data is accomplished with the help of JSON, which stands for JavaScript Object Notation. Working with JSON files is made easier by the 'json' module that is built right into Python.

```python
import json

# Reading a JSON file
with open("data.json", "r") as json_file:
    data = json.load(json_file)
    print(data)

# Writing to a JSON file
data = {"name": "Alice", "age": 25}
with open("new_data.json", "w") as json_file:
    json.dump(data, json_file)
```

Reading and writing binary files is covered in this section.

Data is stored in binary files using a format that is not text. Using the "rb" (read binary) and "wb" (write binary) modes, Python is able to read and write binary data in files.

```python
# Reading a binary file
with open("image.jpg", "rb") as binary_file:
    data = binary_file.read()
    print("Read", len(data), "bytes")

# Writing to a binary file
data = b"Binary data example"
with open("new_binary_file.bin", "wb") as binary_file:
    binary_file.write(data)
```

6.7 Some Final Thoughts

Handling files is a fundamental ability for any coder to possess. Python offers a flexible set of tools that can be used to interact with a variety of file formats, giving one the ability to read and write data in a time-efficient manner. One should keep in mind that one should always correctly close files, that one should gracefully handle exceptions, and that one should use the right file mode for

the requirements. Through consistent practice, one will develop the self-assurance necessary to manage files and integrate them fluidly into the programs.

6.8 Managing File Locations and Paths

It is essential to have an accurate understanding of how to manage file paths if working with files, particularly when interacting with a variety of operating systems. The 'os.path' module of Python offers functions that allow users to work with file paths in a manner that is independent of the platform.

```python
import os

# Joining paths
folder = "data"
file_name = "example.txt"
file_path = os.path.join(folder, file_name)
print("File path:", file_path)

# Getting the basename and dirname
print("Base name:", os.path.basename(file_path))
print("Directory name:", os.path.dirname(file_path))

# Checking if a path exists
if os.path.exists(file_path):
    print("File exists!")
else:
    print("File does not exist.")
```

6.9 Handling Files with the Assistance of Context Managers

In earlier parts of this chapter, individuals read about the opened files by making use of the 'with' statement. Utilizing context managers is the name of this strategy, which comes highly suggested for file management. Context managers are responsible for ensuring that resources are managed appropriately, regardless of whether or not exceptions occur within the block.

```
with open("example.txt", "r") as file:
    content = file.read()
    print(content)
# File is automatically closed when the block is exited
```

6.10 Encoding and the Unicode Standard

It is essential to take into consideration the encoding whilst working with text files. The encoding that is utilized by default by the 'open()' function differs depending on the platform. In order to avoid problems, one can choose to explicitly define the encoding:

```
with open("example.txt", "r") as file:
    content = file.read()
    print(content)
# File is automatically closed when the block is exited
```

Python program with open("file.txt", "r", "encoding="utf-8") as file: content = file.read() prints the content with the "'" character.

Handling files is a fundamental skill in programming because it enables one to interface with data sources that are located outside of one's application. Python has a comprehensive collection of utilities for facilitating the processing of a wide variety of file formats, including text files, CSV files, JSON files, and binary files. One will have greater success reading and writing data from and to files if they are familiar with the various file modes, make use of context managers, and respond appropriately to exceptions. In addition, ensuring that file paths are handled appropriately and taking into account encoding are two essential issues that must be considered in order to provide robust and platform-independent file handling.

Building on the ideas of exception handling presented in the framework of this chapter, the following chapter will be devoted to the study of error handling and exceptions in the Python programming language.

Chapter 7: Error Handling

Python comes with a rich collection of tools that help improve the code's stability and reduce the likelihood of errors and exceptions, which can lead to the failure of a program or unexpected behaviour. Errors and exceptions can cause unexpected behaviour or even prevent a program from running entirely if they are not handled properly. Python offers a wide variety of built-in methods and procedures that can help one deal with problems like these and make one's code more reliable. In this walkthrough, one will become familiar with the various types of errors as well as the built-in methods, complete with examples.

An issue that occurs within a program and prevents the program from completing its mission is referred to as an error. In contrast, the definition of an exception refers to a condition that deviates from the typical operation of the program. Both errors and exceptions belong to the category of runtime errors, which denotes that they manifest themselves when a program is being carried out.

To put it another way, an error is a significant problem that a typical application is not expected to catch, whereas an exception is a situation that a program is expected to capture.

7.1 Types of Errors

Syntax errors and runtime difficulties are the two most common types of Python mistakes.

Errors in Syntax: Syntax errors, also known as processing errors, occur when the Python interpreter encounters a line of code that does not adhere to the language's established syntax rules. The syntax errors are caught during compilation and prevent the program from running until they are rectified. Syntax problems often take the form of simple things like improper indentation, missing colons, or misspelt terms. Here's an example of a syntax error that might occur in Python:

```python
# incorrect indentation
def add_numbers(x, y):
return x + y
```

In the example that was just presented, the function declaration does not contain the necessary indentation, which leads to a syntax error:

```
File "<ipython-input-1-7163263e7970>", line 2
    return x + y
    ^
IndentationError: expected an indented block
```

Runtime Errors: Errors that occur during the execution of a program are referred to as runtime errors. Exceptions are another name for runtime errors. These mistakes may be brought on by a number of different factors, including improper input, incorrect data types, or unexpected action on the part of the application. Runtime mistakes in Python can take many forms, but some of the more common ones include the ZeroDivisionError, ValueError, and TypeError. The following is an example of a runtime mistake that can occur in Python:

```
# dividing a number by zero
a = 10
b = 0
c = a/b
```

This piece of code endeavours to perform a division using the value of the variable a, which is set to 10, and the value of the variable b, which is set to 0. Since division by zero is not a mathematical operation that can be specified, this line of code will produce an error. To be more specific, it will cause Python's ZeroDivisionError to be thrown.

```
ZeroDivisionError                          Traceback (most recent call last)
Cell In[1], line 4
      2 a = 10
      3 b = 0
----> 4 c = a/b

ZeroDivisionError: division by zero
```

Best Practices for Error Handling

- When it comes to the handling of errors in Python, there are a few best practices that one should follow if they want to design code that is more robust and trustworthy. The following are some considerations to keep in mind:

- Handle exceptions at the proper level of abstraction. It is essential, while dealing with exceptions, to take into account the level of abstraction at which the exception occurred. If one has a function that opens a file and reads the content of that file, for instance, it is in one's best interest to handle any problems that may arise when accessing the file or reading the content of the file within the context of that function. This way, one can catch and manage the issue instantly without having to send it up to a higher-level function that might not have enough context to handle the error correctly. One can do this by using the catch keyword.

- Error messages should be clear and informative, offering sufficient information to assist the user or developer in understanding what went wrong and how to correct it. Write error messages that are clear and informative. The message should specify the sort of problem that has occurred, as well as the name of the function or module where the issue was generated, as well as any other pertinent data or context.

- Implement error handling that is consistent across one's code. If one wants their code to be easy to maintain and to debug, they should implement error handling that is consistent throughout one's codebase. This entails applying the same pattern and strategy to the handling of errors across all of the functions and modules that one has.

- Test the code that deals with errors. When one tests their code, make sure to also test the code that deals with errors. This requires testing not just for scenarios in which exceptions are thrown (to verify that their handling is appropriate) but also for scenarios in which exceptions are not thrown (to validate that the program performs as intended under typical circumstances).

- It is essential to document one's error-handling code in order to ensure that other developers, as well as one's own future self, are able to comprehend how mistakes are handled and the reasoning for doing so. Documenting the different kinds of errors that can be thrown, how they are dealt with, and any relevant context or facts is part of this.

- Logging is a helpful tool for tracking mistakes in one's code, so be sure to make advantage of it. The built-in Python logging module allows one to log error messages and other information, which can assist one in debugging problems and monitoring the performance of one's code.

In general, it's best to avoid using bare unless clauses, as they can make it more challenging to track down the source of an error. Using these phrases can lead to ambiguity because they cover every possible scenario. Instead, throw exceptions of known types or catch them at the right abstraction level. Following these guidelines will result in more readable and easily debugged code that is also more manageable, reliable, and resilient.

7.2 Standard Exceptions

The following is a list of the default exceptions in Python, along with their descriptions:

- When the assert statement is invalidated, the AssertionError is generated.

- EOFError is generated if the input() method is called when the end-of-file condition has been satisfied.

- AttributeError is the error that is thrown whenever an attempt to assign or reference an attribute fails.

- TabError is generated whenever the indentation consists of tabs or spaces that are not consistent with one another.

- ImportError is the error that is thrown whenever there is a problem importing the module.

- IndexError is an error that happens when the index of a sequence is outside of the allowed range.

- KeyboardInterrupt is triggered whenever the user presses one of the interrupt keys, such as Ctrl + C or Delete.

- When an error does not fit into any of the other categories, RuntimeError is generated.

- NameError is the exception that is thrown whenever a variable cannot be located in either the local or the global scope.

- MemoryError is the error that is generated when a program has exhausted its memory.

- An instance of ValueError is generated whenever an operation or function is passed an argument that has the correct type but the incorrect value.

- An instance of the ZeroDivisionError exception is thrown whenever a value or variable is divided by zero.

- A SyntaxError is generated by the parser whenever there is an error in the Python syntax.

- An instance of the IndentationError: error message appears whenever the indentation is incorrect.

- SystemError is the error that is thrown when the interpreter finds an error within itself.

- Reading the documentation for Python will provide one with access to a comprehensive list of the language's errors and exceptions.

Handling of Exceptions with the try, except, else, and finally, Statements

Here one will first become familiar with errors and exceptions and then move on to understanding how to handle them by utilizing blocks labelled try, except, otherwise, and finally.

So, what exactly do individuals mean when they say to handle them? In typical situations, the execution of the code will be halted, and an error message will be displayed when one of these issues occurs. One needs to be able to predict these problems and come up with alternate solutions or warning messages so that they can build stable systems.

In this section, individuals will discover what the various building blocks perform and how one can include them in their code to make it more robust.

Try and except Statement

Using the 'try' and 'except' blocks in Python is the simplest method for managing exceptions in this programming language.

- Perform the operation on the code within the 'try' statement.

- Execute the code that is located under the 'except' statement whenever an exception is thrown.

When an error or exception is encountered, the code will continue to search for other possible solutions rather than stopping.

Simple example:

In the first example, there is an attempt to print the variable 'x' even though it is not yet defined. The error should be thrown, and the execution should be halted in typical conditions; however, by utilizing the 'try' and 'except' blocks, one is able to modify the behaviour of the flow.

- The code located within the 'try' statement will be executed by the application.

- Because one already knows that 'x' is not defined, the unless statement will be executed, and a warning will be printed.

```
try:
    print(x)
except:
    print("An exception has occurred!")


    An exception has occurred!
```

```
An exception has occurred!
```

Multiple exceptions to the rule

In the second example, it is demonstrated how to handle a variety of exceptions by utilizing a number of different 'except' statements.

- In the event that a ZeroDivisionError exception is thrown, the application will output the message "You cannot divide a value with zero."

- For the remaining exceptional cases, it will print out the message "Something else went wrong."

It enables one to build flexible code that can handle several exceptions at the same time without causing the program to malfunction.

```
try:
    print(1/0)
except ZeroDivisionError:
    print("You cannot divide a value with zero")
except:
    print("Something else went wrong")
```

```
You cannot divide a value with zero
```

The example file is being loaded.

Here is the CSV file in the following code, and if it throws a FileNotFoundError exception, the code will output the error along with an additional message regarding the 'data.csv' file.

Without interrupting the execution, it is possible to print the default error messages.

```
try:
    with open('data.csv') as file:
        read_data = file.read()
except FileNotFoundError as fnf_error:
    print(fnf_error)
    print("Explanation: We cannot load the 'data.csv' file")
```

```
[Errno 2] No such file or directory: 'data.csv'
Explanation: We cannot load the 'data.csv' file
```

Else Statement

After gaining an understanding of the 'try' and 'except' statements, lets now move on to studying the 'else' statement. The 'else' block is executed by the program when the 'try' statement does not result in an exception being thrown. When one anticipates that a portion of one's script will result in an exception, it is the solution, also known as a fallback option. It is typically employed in a brief setup or verification stage in which one does not want particular faults to remain hidden.

Simple example:

The example of ZeroDivisionError will now include the 'else' statement that is just created. As one can see, the print function located within the 'else' sentence is carried out whenever there are no exceptions, and the output is shown as a consequence of this action.

```
try:
    result = 1/3
except ZeroDivisionError as err:
    print(err)
else:
    print(f"Your answer is {result}")
```

```
Your answer is 0.3333333333333333
```

Example of IndexError with else clause

Let's get some additional knowledge by developing a basic function and putting it through its paces in a number of different situations.

The 'find_nth_value' function takes two arguments: a list, denoted by 'x', and an index number, denoted by 'n'. In order to properly handle the IndexError exception, here is crafted a block consisting of a try, an except, and an otherwise statement.

```
x = [5,8,9,13]

def find_nth_value(x,n):
    try:
        result = x[n]
    except IndexError as err:
        print(err)
    else:
        print("Your answer is ", result)
```

The 'x' list contains four different values, and it is tested using the sixth and second indices.

```
    # Testing
find_nth_value(x,6)
find_nth_value(x,2)
```

At the point where n equalled 6, the IndexError exception was thrown, and here one is presented with the error default message "list index out of range."

At the point where n equaled 2, there was no exception that was thrown, and the function displayed the result that is located within the 'else' expression.

```
list index out of range
Your answer is  9
```

Finally Keyword

In the try-except block, the 'finally' keyword is always executed, regardless of whether or not there is an exception. This is the case even if there is no exception. In plain English, the 'finally' block of code is executed after the try block, with the exception of the otherwise block, which is executed as the final block. It is of great assistance in clearing out resources and shutting down the object, particularly in terms of shutting down files.

The 'divide' method was developed specifically to manage ZeroDivisionError exceptions and to show the result only when there were no other errors. No of the result, it will always run 'finally' to print "Code by DataCamp" in green colour. This will happen regardless of the outcome.

```
def divide(x,y):
    try:
        result = x/y
    except ZeroDivisionError:
        print("Please change 'y' argument to non-zero value")
    except:
        print("Something went wrong")
    else:
        print(f"Your answer is {result}")
    finally:
        print("\033[92m Code by DataCamp\033[00m")
```

In the first test, the programmer is going to divide 1 by 0, which will cause the ZeroDivisionError exception to be thrown and will cause the message to be printed. As can be seen, there is an additional line following the error message in the code.

```
divide(1,0)
```

```
Please change 'y' argument to non-zero value
```

When one adds valid input, it shows the result by executing the 'else' and 'finally' blocking statements and then continuing on to the next step.

```
divide(3,4)
```

```
Your answer is 0.75
 Code by DataCamp
```

When inserted, a string as the second argument rather than an integer, which causes an error to be thrown that is distinct from ZeroDivisionError and has a different message.

```
divide(1,'g')
```

```
Something went wrong
```

There is one aspect that is consistent throughout all three different possibilities. The 'finally' statement will always result in the 'print' function being executed within the code.

7.3 Nested Exception Handling

When one is preparing the software to handle numerous exceptions in a row, they need to use nested exception handling. For instance, one can tack on an additional try-except block directly below the 'else' expression. Therefore, in the event that the first statement does not result in an error, one should check the second statement against the remaining portion of the code.

Adjusting the Function of Divide

One can improve the 'division' function that was demonstrated in the earlier example by including an 'else' line immediately behind a nested try-except block. Therefore, if there is no AttributeError,

it will run the 'else' statement and check the new code for an exception relating to ZeroDivisionError.

```python
def divide(x,y):
    try:
        value = 50
        x.append(value)

    except AttributeError as atr_err:
        print(atr_err)

    else:
        try:
            result = [i / y for i in x]
            print( result )
        except ZeroDivisionError:
            print("Please change 'y' argument to non-zero value")

    finally:
        print("\033[92m Code by DataCamp\033[00m")
```

In the first possible case, one will give one a list of three different values for 'x' and the numerator 3. The script will display the result after first adding 50 to the list, then dividing each value on the list by 3, and finally displaying the new total.

Example of Editing a File

Let's take a look at some additional real-world examples of loading a file, writing content to the file, and closing the file.

- Examine the 'open()' function's FileNotFoundError error for more information.

- In the event that the outer exception does not be thrown, it will examine the 'write()' function exception.

- No matter what happens, once the file has been opened, it will immediately close itself by executing the 'finally' line.

- In the event that the outer try statement throws an exception, the program will give an erroneous file path in the error message that it returns.

Nested exception handling is not recommended because it adds unnecessary complexity; instead, developers should utilize many try-except blocks to provide sequential, easy-to-understand exception processing.

Chapter 8: Python Libraries

Python, a programming language that is both flexible and powerful, owes a significant portion of its appeal to the vast range of libraries that are made available to developers. These libraries are pre-written bundles of code that offer a variety of functionalities. By utilizing these libraries, developers are able to simplify their work and more effectively handle complex problems. Readers will delve into the world of Python libraries, gain a knowledge of their value, and then explore some of the essential ones in detail as one proceeds through this complete introduction.

8.1 Overview of Popular Python Libraries

"Batteries included" is the tagline of the Python programming language, which highlights the company's dedication to providing a comprehensive standard library with the language itself. The actual power of Python, however, lies in the third-party libraries that are developed by the Python community. These libraries improve Python's ability to cover a wide variety of activities, ranging from web development and data analysis to machine learning and artificial intelligence. Among the jobs that can be addressed by Python as a result of these libraries is artificial intelligence. The value of Python libraries resides in their capacity to save both time and effort, to encourage the reusability of code, and to facilitate collaboration between software developers.

Types of Python Libraries:

The functions that Python libraries are able to perform allow for the broad classification of these resources into a variety of fields. The following are some of the most important categories:

Web Development: Libraries such as Flask and Django simplify the process of developing web applications by taking care of routing, templating, and other essential capabilities.

Data Manipulation and Analysis: Libraries such as NumPy, pandas, and Matplotlib give tools for data manipulation, analysis, and visualization. These libraries are essential for data scientists and analysts because of the capabilities they provide.

Machine Learning: Tools for machine learning and deep learning are provided by libraries such as scikit-learn, TensorFlow, and PyTorch. These libraries enable software developers to construct and train complex models.

Natural Language Processing (NLP) refers to the processing and analysis of human language made possible by libraries such as NLTK and spaCy. This paves the way for applications such as sentiment analysis and language production.

Game Development: Libraries such as Pygame provide support for game development by providing tools for the creation of experiences that are both interactive and immersive.

Networking: Libraries such as queries make it easier to send HTTP queries, and Twisted provides a framework for developing applications that make use of many networks.

Scientific Computing: Libraries such as SciPy provide functionality for scientific and mathematical computing, including optimization, integration, and linear algebra. This functionality is used in the field of scientific computing.

In the field of cybersecurity, libraries like Paramiko provide secure communication using SSH, which helps in the development of secure network applications.

Data Storage and Databases: Libraries such as SQLAlchemy help facilitate the process of dealing with databases and provide an abstraction layer for the purpose of data management.

Most Important Python Libraries:

- NumPy is the Python library that serves as the basis for numerical and scientific computing in the language. It does this by presenting the ndarray, which is an n-dimensional array This makes it possible to efficiently store and manipulate matrices and arrays. Data analysis and scientific computing would be impossible without it because of its mathematical operations, its ability to generate random numbers, and its integration with other libraries.

- Pandas is a toolkit for data manipulation and analysis that provides several data structures, such as Series and DataFrame. It is particularly effective in managing structured data and carrying out operations such as filtering, grouping, and aggregating the results. Pandas make it much easier to complete activities related to the preparation of data, making it an essential tool for data scientists.

- When it comes to the visualization of data, the Matplotlib package is an excellent resource to have. It offers a diverse selection of charting choices, ranging from straightforward line plots and scatter plots to complex visualizations. Its connection with NumPy and pandas makes it possible to represent data without any interruptions.

- Scikit-learn is a virtual treasure trove for people who are passionate about machine learning. This library provides a variety of machine learning algorithms in addition to tools for data preprocessing, model selection, and evaluation. Because of its intuitive user interface, it is a good place for newbies to the industry to begin their studies.

- Google's TensorFlow is widely regarded as the most successful open-source library for deep learning. TensorFlow was developed by Google. It gives programmers the ability to construct and train neural networks to perform a variety of tasks, including image recognition, natural language processing, and more. Because of its adaptability and support for processing on both CPUs and GPUs, it has become an essential component in AI research.

- PyTorch: In direct competition with TensorFlow, PyTorch has been gaining traction thanks to its user-friendly interface and dynamic computational graph. It is particularly liked by researchers and developers that desire a greater degree of control over the architecture of models when they are experimenting with and developing them.

- The Natural Language Toolkit, sometimes known as NLTK, is an invaluable resource for those who work in the field of NLP. It comes with a plethora of text corpora and resources for NLP research, as well as tools for tokenization, stemming, and parsing.

- When it comes to the creation of websites, the micro-framework known as Flask is particularly useful. It's not only lightweight but also simple to understand, and it makes it possible for developers to rapidly design web apps. Because of its ease of use and ability to be extended, it is frequently selected for use in startups and other relatively modest projects.

- On the opposite end of the spectrum is Django, which is a full-stack web framework that provides a solid foundation for the construction of large and feature-rich web applications. Django is an example of a web application. It adheres to the principle of "batteries included" and provides built-in administrative panels, authentication, and other features.

- Making HTTP requests is a typical operation in web development, and the Requests library streamlines this process by reducing the amount of work that is required. It offers a sophisticated and user-friendly application programming interface (API) for delivering HTTP requests and managing answers.

- The sophisticated NLP library known as spaCy places an emphasis on both effectiveness and velocity in its operations. It provides models that have already been pre-trained for a variety of languages, which makes it possible to do tasks such as named entity recognition, part-of-speech tagging, and syntax parsing. Because of the library's focus on efficiency, it is often the tool of choice for natural language processing pipelines that must execute in real-time or on a massive scale.

- Pygame is a cross-platform toolkit that makes it easy for game developers to construct 2D games. Pygame is referred to as "Pygame." It has functions for dealing with images and audio as well as input from the user. Pygame is frequently suggested to novice programmers just starting out in the game development industry because of the ease of use and depth of its documentation.

- Twisted is a well-established and well-recognized library that specializes in the development of network applications. It provides an event-driven programming approach, which makes it appropriate for use in the construction of asynchronous network servers and clients. Developers have a tool at their disposal in Twisted that makes it easier for them to design scalable and responsive network applications.

- SciPy: Whereas NumPy is primarily concerned with arrays, SciPy expands NumPy's functionality by offering access to a wider variety of scientific and mathematical operations. It comes with modules that can optimize, integrate, interpolate, and perform signal processing, among other functions. SciPy, in conjunction with NumPy, constitutes a full suite for the performance of tasks related to scientific computing.

- The term "Paramiko" refers to a library that, among other things, makes it easier to communicate securely using SSH (Secure Shell) protocols. It gives developers the ability to create SSH clients and servers, which enables safe remote access to systems and management of those systems. Tasks that entail automating remote server activities are ideally suited for use with Paramiko because of its many useful capabilities.

- Through the use of SQLAlchemy, working with databases may become both more intuitive and adaptable. Working with relational databases is made easier with the help of this Object-Relational Mapping (ORM) library, which features an abstraction layer. It makes tasks such as creating database schemas, querying databases, and manipulating data much simpler while giving compatibility with a variety of database management systems.

- Beautiful Soup: Web scraping, often known as the process of obtaining information from websites, is an area in which Beautiful Soup shines. It is capable of parsing HTML and XML documents, which makes it simple to explore online pages and obtain data from them. When combined with libraries such as Requests, Beautiful Soup makes it easier to successfully complete web scraping applications.

- Asynchronous programming is essential to the development of highly responsive apps that are able to manage several processes in parallel. One is able to construct asynchronous code by using coroutines thanks to the event loop that is provided by the asyncio package. This makes it possible to have efficient concurrent I/O operations that do not block.

- The multiprocessing library in Python gives programmers the ability to make efficient use of computers with many CPU cores. It offers a user interface for the creation of parallel processes, which enables one to take advantage of the power of modern processors for activities that may be broken down into multiple independent units of work.

- Seaborn is built on top of Matplotlib and provides a higher-level interface for the purpose of producing statistical visualizations that are aesthetically pleasant. It makes data discovery and communication more straightforward by simplifying the production of complicated visualizations such as heatmaps, violin plots, and pair plots.

- Plotly is a library that may be used in a variety of ways to create interactive and dynamic data representations. It is especially helpful for making interactive graphs that can be incorporated into online apps or presentations, and it supports a broad variety of chart kinds.

- Requests is not only a flexible library for making HTTP requests, but it is also an essential component for dealing with web APIs. Requests were written by the Requests project. Tasks like sending GET and POST requests, handling headers, and processing results are made easier as a result.

- Despite the fact that it is not a third-party library, the built-in support for JSON (JavaScript Object Notation) in Python is something that should be pointed out. The JSON data exchange format is a lightweight format that is commonly used for web APIs as well as configuration files. The native support that Python has for JSON serialization and deserialization makes it much easier for apps to exchange data with one another.

- Dask is a helpful tool to have when working with enormous datasets that cannot be stored in memory at the same time. Using a syntax that is similar to that of Pandas, it offers features for parallel computing that may be applied to activities such as the processing, aggregation, and filtering of data.

- GeoPandas enhances the capabilities of Pandas for the purpose of geospatial data analysis. It does this by adding support for spatial data types and operations. It is a useful tool for working with geospatial data since it makes it possible to complete tasks such as geocoding, spatial joins, and map visualizations.

- Python Imaging Library, or PIL for short: PIL, which can alternatively be referred to as Pillow, is a sophisticated library that can be used to work with images. It enables users to perform operations such as manipulating images, resizing them, applying filters, and more. PIL is utilized extensively in activities such as image preprocessing for machine learning and the development of applications that are picture-centric.

- Pmdarima: the study of time series data frequently includes activities such as forecasting and the discovery of anomalies. For the purpose of time series forecasting, the pmdarima library makes the process of selecting and tuning AutoRegressive Integrated Moving Average (ARIMA) models more straightforward.

8.2 NumPy for Numerical Computing

A comprehensive look at Python's fundamental array library, numpy, with applications in numerical computing.

NumPy is an acronym that stands for "Numerical Python," and it is widely considered to be one of the most important building blocks for scientific and numerical computing in Python. This robust library offers support for big, multi-dimensional arrays and matrices, in addition to a wide variety of mathematical functions that may be utilized to perform efficient operations on these arrays. During this in-depth investigation, individuals will delve into the inner workings and relevance of NumPy, studying its fundamental characteristics, array manipulation capabilities, and role in scientific computing.

Arrays and their benefits.

The ndarray, often known as an n-dimensional array, is the data structure that NumPy considers to be its most essential component. In contrast to Python's built-in lists, ndarrays provide a number of important benefits, including the following:

- Homogeneous Data: Arrays include members of the same data type, which ensures constant performance and memory utilization. Arrays can also be thought of as having a homogeneous data structure.

- Memory Efficiency: NumPy arrays have excellent memory efficiency because they store data in contiguous memory blocks, which reduces the amount of memory overhead that must be maintained.

- Vectorized Operations: NumPy's vectorized operations make it possible to do calculations on elements one at a time without the need for explicit looping, which results in faster execution speeds.

- In the realm of broadcasting: NumPy can conduct operations on arrays of varying forms thanks to broadcasting, which also aligns the dimensions of the arrays so that calculations may be performed more quickly.

The creation of arrays and their manipulation:

The construction of NumPy arrays is a simple process. One can start arrays by using Python lists or nested lists, and NumPy includes functions such as 'numpy.array()' and 'numpy.zeros()' to generate arrays of certain shapes and values, respectively. In addition, the 'arange()' and 'linspace()' functions that are included in NumPy are helpful when it comes to the generation of number sequences.

NumPy's capabilities are broken down into several categories, one of which being array manipulation. The library provides access to a comprehensive set of functions for reshaping, slicing, and indexing arrays in a variety of formats. While indexing makes it possible to have immediate access to particular components or subsets, slicing permits the extraction of specified subsets of data from arrays. Not only are these activities effective, but they are also important for the preliminary processing and examination of data.

The Relationship Between Mathematical Functions and Broadcasting:

The breadth and depth of NumPy's support for mathematical operations is one of the software's most notable strengths. NumPy can assist individuals with any type of mathematical calculation, from the most fundamental arithmetic operations to the most complex mathematical computations. Arrays can have element-wise operations performed on them via functions like 'numpy.add()', 'numpy.subtract()', 'numpy.multiply()', and 'numpy.divide()'. These functions provide a syntax that is both clean and effective.

The broadcasting feature is one of the most notable aspects of NumPy. One can able to perform operations between arrays that have varied shapes and dimensions by utilizing broadcasting. This aligns the arrays in such a way that calculations may be carried out without the need for explicit looping. This feature makes complicated processes easier to understand, decreases the need for nested loops, and improves the readability of the code.

A Statistical Breakdown and Aggregation of the Data:

Aggregating data and conducting statistical analysis on arrays are two of NumPy's strong suits. Functions such as 'numpy.sum()', 'numpy.mean()', 'numpy.median()', and 'numpy.std()' offer insights into the distribution and features of one's data. These processes are extremely important for data analysis, and they may be carried out effectively even on very big datasets.

Efficiency and optimizations are as follows:

NumPy is designed from the ground up to be as productive as possible. Because so many of its fundamental operations are programmed in low-level languages such as C and Fortran, the software always runs quickly and efficiently. In the field of scientific computing, where performing operations on big datasets can be quite computationally intensive, this performance is of especially crucial importance.

Integration with Various Other Libraries

NumPy is the backbone around which a variety of different scientific libraries written in Python are built. NumPy's array structure serves as the foundation for the libraries SciPy, pandas, and scikit-learn, which offer specialized functionality for scientific computing, data analysis, and machine learning, respectively.

8.3 Pandas for Data Analysis

A paradigm shift may be seen in the field of data manipulation and analysis as a result of the Pandas package. Pandas streamline the process of dealing with structured data thanks to its robust set of tools and user-friendly syntax. As a result, it has become an indispensable tool for data scientists, analysts, and researchers. During this in-depth investigation, individuals are going to delve into the fundamental capabilities of Pandas, gaining a grasp of their data structures, their capacities for manipulating data, and their central position in the processes of data analysis.

Introducing Pandas:

The Series and the DataFrame are the two primary data structures that form the foundation of the Pandas framework. The Series is a one-dimensional labelled array, but the DataFrame is a two-dimensional table that is similar to a spreadsheet or a SQL table. Both of these tables are used for data analysis. Pandas' data analysis skills are built on top of these data structures, which provide a structured way to store and manipulate data and serve as the framework for those capabilities.

Loading and Inspecting Data:

Pandas make it possible to import data from a wide variety of sources using a selection of different techniques. These methods include importing data from CSV files, Excel spreadsheets, SQL databases, and even online APIs. The utilities 'pandas.read_csv()', 'pandas.read_excel()', and 'pandas.read_sql()' make the process of loading data into a Pandas DataFrame more straightforward.

After the data has been loaded, Pandas gives users a wide variety of options to evaluate and investigate the data. Functions such as 'head()' and 'tail()', as well as 'info()' and 'description()', provide insights into the structure, data types, and summary statistics of the dataset.

Data Cleaning and Preprocessing:

Cleaning and preparing the data constitutes a sizeable percentage of the whole data analysis process. Pandas excel in this area because it has tools that can manage missing values, duplicate entries, and inconsistent data. Methods such as 'dropna()', 'fillna()', 'drop_duplicates()', and'replace()' make it possible to clean and prepare data quickly and effectively.

Data Manipulation and Transformation:

The real strength of Pandas lies in their capacity to manipulate and alter data in various ways. Pandas provides one with a syntax that is condensed yet expressive, making it possible to execute operations such as filtering, sorting, grouping, and aggregation. The 'groupby()' and 'pivot_table()' functions allow for the grouping of data based on specified columns and the application of aggregation functions, respectively, while the 'pivot_table()' function gives sophisticated capabilities for pivoting data.

Indexing and Selection:

Pandas provides a wide variety of methods that can be used to select and index data included within DataFrames. In order to isolate particular subsets of data, one can make use of labels, indexing that is based on integers, and even boolean conditions. The accessor methods 'loc[]' and 'iloc[]' make it possible to choose and modify data with a high degree of accuracy.

Merging and Joining Data:

Pandas have functions to merge and connect DataFrames, which can be helpful when working with different datasets. The'merge()' function enables one to combine datasets based on similar columns or indices. This functionality is available regardless of whether one is doing an inner, outer, left, or right join.

Time Series Analysis:

Pandas have powerful facilities for managing date and time-related operations, which can be used for processing time series data. Pandas is an ideal choice for studying time series datasets because of the 'Timestamp' and 'DatetimeIndex' classes, which provide smooth manipulation of time-based data.

Data Visualization:

Although data visualization is not Pandas' major focus, the library interfaces quite well with other data visualization tools like Matplotlib and Seaborn. The 'plot()' function of Pandas makes it possible to generate exploratory charts directly from DataFrames, which simplifies the process of constructing basic visualizations.

Python's ability to manage and analyze data has been greatly improved with the introduction of the versatile Pandas library. Because of its intuitive interface and comprehensive collection of features for manipulating data, it is a useful companion for data professionals. Pandas accelerate the whole data analysis workflow, from data cleaning and preprocessing to advanced analysis and visualization. This frees up critical time for more meaningful insights and decision-making.

Learning how to use Pandas is a requirement for anyone who works with data, regardless of their level of experience in the field of data science. If one delves deeper into its operations and features, it will be able to uncover new dimensions of data exploration and manipulation. Pandas is a reliable Swiss Army Knife as one navigates the huge sea of data. It is prepared to solve the most complicated data analysis issues with elegance and efficiency.

8.4 Matplotlib for Data Visualization

Matplotlib is widely regarded as the go-to toolkit for data visualization thanks to its extensive range of features and capabilities. Matplotlib is an essential part of the Python ecosystem. It allows data scientists, analysts, and researchers to build visually engaging and instructive representations of their data. During this condensed examination, individuals will get to the heart of Matplotlib by grasping its fundamental features, plot types, customisation possibilities, and its use in illuminating patterns and insights hidden inside data.

Introduction to Matplotlib:

Matplotlib is a library for charting in two dimensions that offers a comprehensive set of tools for generating various charts, graphs, and plots. Matplotlib provides the tools necessary to show data in meaningful ways, regardless of whether one is working with straightforward line plots, elaborate scatter plots, or intricate bar charts.

Core Components and Plotting Basics:

The 'pyplot' module and the 'Figure' and 'Axes' objects are the two primary building blocks upon which Matplotlib is constructed. A high level interface for creating and managing plots is provided by the 'pyplot' module, where the 'Figure' represents the overall plotting area and the 'Axes' represents specific plot areas included within the figure.

Using Matplotlib, generating a simple plot is a simple and uncomplicated process. One is able to produce a wide variety of visualizations by importing the 'pyplot' module and then using functions such as 'plot()','scatter()', and 'bar()'. Personalizing features like labels, titles, and legends can improve the plots' visual clarity and their ability to communicate information effectively.

Common Plot Types:

Matplotlib provides support for a wide variety of plot types, which enables data visualization in many different areas, including the following:

- Line Plots are perfect for illustrating patterns and trends across continuous data points.

- Scatter Plots are useful for demonstrating the connections and correlations that exist between two different variables.

- Bar Charts are helpful for comparing categorical data as well as displaying distributions across categories.

- Histograms are helpful for visualizing frequency distributions and comprehending the distribution of data.

- Pie Charts are useful for displaying relationships between parts and the whole as well as proportions.

- Box Plots are informative charts that can be used to visualize data distributions and locate outliers in the data.

- Heatmaps are an indispensable tool for visually visualizing data matrices through the use of colour-coded values.

Customization and Styling:

The adaptability of Matplotlib is highlighted by the numerous customisation possibilities it provides. One has the ability to personalize their plots by changing the colours, line styles, marker positions, and typefaces. While the 'set()' and 'rcParams' functions let one establish global plot settings, the 'subplot()' function lets one create numerous plots within a single figure. Both of these functions are located in the 'plot' and 'figure' namespaces.

Annotations and Interactivity:

The communication value of plots created using Matplotlib is significantly increased by the addition of annotations and interactivity. Annotations in the form of text, arrows, and shapes can be added to the chart in order to draw attention to particular data points. In addition, the interaction capabilities of Matplotlib make it possible to zoom in and out, pan around, and save plot parts as either pictures or vector graphics.

Integration with Data Analysis:

Other data analysis libraries, such as NumPy and Pandas, can be easily and seamlessly integrated with Matplotlib. One may take advantage of the powerful data manipulation capabilities of NumPy arrays and Pandas DataFrames by plotting NumPy arrays and Pandas DataFrames directly.

Saving and Exporting:

Matplotlib gives one the option to save their plots in a variety of formats, such as PNG, JPEG, PDF, and SVG, after one's visualizations are complete and ready to be viewed. Because of this versatility, one's visualizations may be incorporated into presentations, reports, and web apps without any problems.

It is impossible to overestimate the importance of Matplotlib in relation to data visualization. A defining characteristic of its usefulness is that it is able to convert unprocessed data into relevant insights by providing a diverse range of plot formats and possibilities for customization. One can uncover patterns, relationships, and trends in one's data by combining the power of Matplotlib with subject expertise. This makes it a vital tool for data-driven decision-making, exploration, and communication. Matplotlib is a reliable friend that helps one paint one's data tales with clarity and power, regardless of whether one is a beginner or an expert.

Chapter 9: Web Development with Flask

The creation of dynamic and interactive websites can be facilitated with the use of Flask for web development. Flask is a micro web framework for Python that gives developers the ability to construct dependable web applications in a relatively straightforward manner. The process of developing web-based solutions using Flask consists of numerous important steps, all of which contribute in their own way to the overall procedure.

9.1 Introduction to Web Development

Web development, at its most fundamental level, entails the creation of programs that can be accessed via the internet. The foundation consists of having an understanding of both the client-side and the server-side components of a web application. The server-side oversees data processing, storage, and logic, whereas the client-side is responsible for what users view and interact with in their browsers.

9.2 Setting up Flask

The installation of Flask is the first step in learning web development. Installing Flask requires the use of tools such as "pip," followed by the creation of a Flask app instance and the adjustment of configurations. The ease of use of Flask is highlighted when the 'app.run()' command is executed because this opens the development server and makes the application viewable in a web browser.

9.3 Creating Web Routes

Web routes are what determine how various URLs can be directed to various components of an application. Decorators are utilized in the process of route definition in Flask. The '@app.route()' decorator attaches a function to a URL. This gives one the ability to describe what occurs when a user reaches a certain route by defining what one wants to happen when they do so. The modularity and maintainability of the system are both improved as a result of this separation of interests.

9.4 Rendering Templates and Forms

One web application will have more structure and style as a result of using templates. In order to generate dynamic HTML, Flask makes use of Jinja2, a strong templating engine. This is accomplished by embedding Python code within HTML files. One is able to present the data from

one's application in a dynamic manner thanks to its dynamic capabilities. Forms, an essential component of user interaction, make it easier for users to submit data. Flask-WTF makes the development and handling of forms much easier, which helps with validating user input.

9.5 Handling Form Data and User Input

Input from users is essential to the functioning of web applications. The request object in Flask is responsible for collecting user submissions, including form data, query parameters, and more. Flask provides one with the tools necessary to ensure that user interactions are both easy and safe. These tools can be used to retrieve, validate, and process data.

To summarize, using Flask for web development provides a more organized approach to the process of developing modern web applications. Understanding of both the frontend and backend components of web development is achieved through the progression of steps beginning with the introduction and ending with the management of user input. By becoming proficient in Flask, developers can give life to their imaginative concepts and construct web apps tailored to the requirements and tastes of individual users. Because of its flexibility, Flask gives pme the ability to confidently negotiate the complexities of web development, regardless of whether they are developing a straightforward blog or an intricate e-commerce platform.

Chapter 10: After Python

With Python skills under one's belt, one can explore a wide variety of career paths in the dynamic field of software engineering.

10.1 Next Steps in Python Learning

After becoming proficient in the principles of Python, one will be able to access a whole new universe of opportunities in the area of programming. One has arrived at a fork in the road and is prepared to make a decision that will lead them to become a better and more flexible developer. One's trip into a world of more complexity and innovation will take shape according to the steps that they take in the coming moments.

If one wants to hone their Python skills, they should investigate more complex ideas and libraries, which will raise the bar for one's coding abilities:

Iterators and Generators:

If one wants to process enormous datasets in a seamless manner, using iterators and generators can help one become an expert in the art of efficiently using memory.

Decorators:

It is important to have a solid understanding of how decorators improve the modularity if code and allow functions to alter other functions, which makes jobs such as logging and authentication much easier.

Exploring metaclasses is a great way to obtain a more in-depth understanding of the process of class formation and regulate the behaviour of classes.

Learn how to manage numerous tasks at once with the help of concurrent programming and multitasking by reading up on concurrency and multithreading.modules for the future.

Asynchronous Programming:

Optimize I/O-bound activities and network operations by delving into asynchronous programming using async and await. Asynchronous programming.

Context Managers:

Utilize the with a statement to one's advantage by adopting context managers for improved resource management and cleaner code.

Advanced-Data Structures Investigate increasingly elaborate data structures such as trees, graphs, and heaps in order to solve increasingly difficult algorithmic challenges.

Software Design Patterns:

Familiarize oneself with design patterns that will assist one in producing code that is scalable, manageable, and effective:

- The Singleton Pattern teaches individuals how to make sure a class has only one instance and how to give a point of access to that instance that can be accessed globally.

- Learn how to create a publish-subscribe mechanism so that numerous objects can be notified when the state of the system changes using the Observer Pattern.

- The Factory Pattern encourages developers to create objects using factory methods and abstract factories rather than explicitly naming the target class.

- The first step in the Strategy Pattern is to discover how to build an algorithm family, encapsulate those algorithms, and make them interchangeable.

- Learn how to change one class's interface into another one clients anticipate using the Adapter Pattern.

Version Control and Collaboration:

If one wants to broaden one's skill set, one should become proficient in using version control systems like Git. Get familiar with the concepts of branching, merging, and working with other people on codebases by using services such as GitHub and GitLab.

Unit Testing and Test-Driven Development (TDD):

Raise the overall quality of one's code by being familiar with the process of writing automated tests using frameworks such as unittest or pytest. Investigate test-driven development, a methodology in which tests are written before the real code is written.

Profiling and Optimization:

Become familiar with the process of analyzing the performance of one's code and locating bottlenecks. Utilize tools such as cProfile to assist in improving the speed and effectiveness of one's code.

Web development:

Front-End Development requires knowledge of HTML, CSS, and JavaScript in order to create user interfaces that are responsive and interactive.

Back-End Development:

To construct strong and dynamic web applications, one needs to become familiar with web frameworks such as Django and Flask.

RESTful APIs:

Become an expert at creating and consuming RESTful APIs to facilitate communication between the various components.

Immersing oneself in data science and machine learning is the key to unlocking the power of data.

Data Science and Machine Learning:

Analyze the data by utilizing data manipulation, exploration, and visualization libraries such as NumPy and pandas.

Learn about supervised and unsupervised learning, model evaluation, and hyperparameter tuning as one delves into machine learning techniques.

Deep Learning requires that one educate oneself on neural networks, namely convolutional neural networks (CNNs) and recurrent neural networks (RNNs), as well as frameworks such as TensorFlow and PyTorch.

Internet of Things (IoT) and Embedded Systems:

Explore the convergence of software and hardware by looking into the development of IoT and embedded systems:

Arduino and Raspberry Pi:

Experiment with programming single-board computers and microcontrollers like Raspberry Pi and Arduino. Arduino is a popular microcontroller.

Sensors and Actuators:

Learn how to control actuators and interact with sensors so that one may construct projects that are applicable in the real world.

Ethical Hacking and Cybersecurity Dive into the area of cybersecurity to gain an understanding of vulnerabilities and to defend systems:

- Network security requires one to educate oneself on firewalls, encryption, and network protocols to protect one's communications.

- Penetration Testing involves investigating various methods of ethical hacking in order to locate and address flaws in security.

- Embrace cloud platforms such as AWS, Azure, or Google Cloud in order to deploy apps when it comes to cloud computing and DevOps:

- Infrastructure as Code (IaC) entails familiarizing oneself with tools such as Terraform to automate the provisioning process.

- Learning Docker to package apps and Kubernetes to orchestrate containerized environments is essential for containerization.

More Advanced Subjects:

Investigate specific fields so that one can expand their skill set:

- Natural Language Processing (NLP) refers to the development of applications that are able to comprehend and produce human language.

- Blockchain technology, smart contracts, and decentralized apps (dApps) are important concepts to get familiar with in relation to cryptocurrency.

- Quantum Computing: Become familiar with the fundamentals of quantum computing as well as the potential applications of this emerging field.

Contributions to Open Source Projects and Personal Projects:

Contribute to open-source projects in order to increase one's visibility in the community, learn from more experienced engineers, and provide value back to the open-source software development ecosystem. Always be working on personal projects to demonstrate how one can apply one's knowledge and improve their talents.

Development of Soft Skills and Career Advancement:

The development of soft skills is vital for the progression of a career:

- One's capacity to clearly convey technical topics to both technical and non-technical audiences should be improved as part of their communication skills.

- Problem-Solving: If one wants to be successful in overcoming difficult difficulties, hone one's problem-solving skills.

- Effective time management requires striking a balance between one's personal life, one's work life, and both.

- Networking is going to events such as conferences, workshops, and meetings to connect with other experts in one's industry.

Teaching and Mentoring:

If one has information to share, they can do it by instructing others, writing tutorials, or assisting others who are just beginning their programming careers.

Maintain a Curious Mindset and Never Stop Learning:

Given the rapid pace at which technology advances, it is important to always be open to new information and never stop learning. Investigate developing linguistic and technological paradigms as well as technologies.

Moving beyond the fundamentals of Python is an exciting adventure that will take one into a wide variety of programming worlds. Individuals will evolve from proficient Pythonista into a versatile and adept developers capable of designing new solutions to complicated challenges if they embrace advanced concepts and specialized domains and make a commitment to continual learning. This will allow one to move beyond the limitations of Python. Therefore, move forward in the world of programming brilliance with self-assurance, completely submerge oneself in the learning process, and carve out a unique route for oneself. One's potential is limitless, and the journey is only beginning.

10.2 Real-World Projects and Challenges

After one has gotten the hang of Python, there are a ton of projects and challenges out there in the real world that one can take on to further improve one's skills. Here is a collection of one hundred ideas that cover a wide range of topics and ability levels:

Web Development:

- Create a website for one's personal portfolio.

- Using Django or Flask, create a blog for one's website.

- Construct a framework for online shopping.

- Conceive a platform for social media.

- Create an application for real-time chatting.

- Construct a program for the management of tasks.

- Create a website that provides weather forecasts.

- Create a tool that can shorten long URLs.

- Develop a service's RESTful application programming interface.

- Create a platform for blogging that supports user authentication.

Data Science and Machine Learning:

- Conduct an analysis of a dataset in order to gain insights and create visuals.

- Construct a technique for analyzing sentiments.

- Create a method for making recommendations.

- Anticipate the movements of the stock market.

- Develop a system for sorting legitimate emails from junk.

- Construct an app that can recognize images.

- Construct a system that can recognize the speaker's voice.

- Create a chatbot for the website.

- Construct a model for predicting the loss of customers.

- Design a game that is based on machine learning.

Automation:

- Create an organizer for one's files that groups them according to their respective types.

- Make a timetable for one's social media accounts.

- Construct a program for scraping websites.

- Create a program that can send emails automatically.

- Create an image resizer that works in batches.

- Construct a mechanism for backing up data.

- Write a script to automate mundane operations in order to save time.

- Create a method for the automation of the document generation process.

- Construct an attendance tracking system.

- Develop a program that can automatically fill out internet forms.

Utilities:

- Create a mobile application for a calculator.

- Establish a unit conversion system.

- Create a random password generator.

- Create a program that functions as a notepad.

- Develop an app for a dictionary.

- Construct a timer with a countdown function.

- Conceive a straightforward game, such as Tic-Tac-Toe.

- Construct a Morse code translator (number 38).

- Construct a currency conversion tool.

- Create a tool that generates quotes at random.

Mobile App Development:

- Develop an app for managing one's to-do list.

- Create an app for keeping track of one's spending.

- Create an app for monitoring one's fitness progress.

- Develop an app for storing and sharing recipes.

- Create an app for learning a foreign language.

- Develop a mobile application for meditation or mindfulness.

- Develop an application for editing photographs.

- Create an application for music streaming.

- Construct a location-based mobile application (for example, a map or a navigational tool).

- Develop an app that can scan barcodes.

Games and Graphics:

- Create a game that involves navigating through mazes.

- Make a game that is a platformer.

- Construct a game, including a puzzle.

- Conceive and create a basic role-playing game (RPG).

- Construct a simulation that is based on physics.

- Construct a graphics engine in either 2D or 3D.

- Using the Pygame programming language, create a game.

- Construct a maze-making and -solving program.

- Create a game that involves tower defence.

- Create a video game with a game engine such as Unity (using Python in conjunction with Unity's API).

IoT and Hardware Projects:

- Creating a home automation system should be step number

- Construct a monitor for the temperature and humidity.

- Create an alarm system that is based on motion sensors.

- Create a doorbell that uses smart technology.

- Construct a weather station with the Internet of Things devices.

- Develop a sophisticated irrigation system for one's garden.

- Establish a monitoring system for the energy used in the residence.

- Construct an automobile or drone that can be commanded remotely.

- Create a fitness tracker that may be worn on the body.

- Install a camera surveillance system in one's home.

Artificial Intelligence and Neural Networks:

- Creating a neural style transfer application is the 71st step.

- Develop a system capable of recognizing handwriting.

- Create an artificial intelligence that can generate music or images.

- Construct a program that summarizes texts.

- Develop a language translation tool powered by artificial intelligence.

- Create a chatbot powered by AI that is capable of understanding natural language.

- Construct a recommendation system that is based on AI.

- Develop an image enhancer that AI drives.

- Create a diagnostic tool for the medical field that AI powers.

- Construct a project involving deep learning by utilizing TensorFlow or PyTorch.

Blockchain and Cryptocurrency:

- Construct a straightforward application of the blockchain.

- Construct an application for monitoring the price of cryptocurrencies.

- Conceive a decentralized voting method.

- Make a program that can be used as a digital signature.

- Construct an application for managing smart contracts.

- Create a tracker for one's cryptocurrency investment portfolio.

- Construct an authentication system that is based on tokens.

- Utilizing blockchain technology, construct a tracking system for supply chains.

- Developing a safe file-sharing application with blockchain.

- Make a decentralized market instead of a centralized one.

Augmented Reality (AR) and Virtual Reality (VR):

- Create an augmented reality app for visualization of interior design.

- Creating an AR-based navigation system should be one's 92nd priority.

- Create a virtual reality (VR) training simulation. 93.

- Create an augmented reality scavenger hunt game.

- Develop an augmented reality art gallery environment.

- Create a virtual reality (VR) instructional app.

- Create an augmented reality-based language-learning app.

- Develop an augmented reality travel guide.

- Create virtual reality software for meditation and relaxation.

- Create an augmented reality (AR) application that allows users to virtually try on clothing.

Always keep in mind that selecting projects that present a challenge while also catering to one's personal passions is the surest path to effective learning and development of skills. One should begin with projects that are appropriate for one's present level of skill and gradually advance to ones that are more difficult as one's experience level increases. Additionally, don't be afraid to blend concepts from a variety of fields in order to produce products that are original and cutting-edge!

Conclusion

Python, a programming language that is well-known for having a syntax that is simple to understand and that is versatile, has become an essential component of the contemporary digital world. Its design philosophy, which places emphasis on readability and simplicity, is responsible for its meteoric climb to prominence. The idea that Guido van Rossum should create a language that "bridges the gap between human thought and machine execution" has struck a chord with developers all around the world and made it easier for them to quickly comprehend concepts and work together effectively. The particular attributes of Python, such as its simple syntax, dynamic typing, and vast standard library, have all played a role in the programming language's meteoric rise to prominence. Because of these traits, developers are able to rapidly prototype, easily adapt to changing requirements, and complete complicated jobs with minimal code.

The influence of Python on the field of software development may be seen throughout a wide variety of subfields. When it comes to web development, frameworks such as Django and Flask, have changed the process of creating dynamic and interactive websites. This has made the process accessible to web developers with varied degrees of expertise. Because of libraries such as NumPy, pandas, and matplotlib, experts are now able to manage, analyze, and visualize data without any hiccups when using this language. This is evidence of the language's stronghold in data science and analytics. Python's integration with machine learning and artificial intelligence, as demonstrated by libraries like TensorFlow and PyTorch, has been a driving force behind recent advances in artificial intelligence. These advancements have ushered in a new era of automation and problem-solving.

There is a flourishing community that is both active and supportive within the blooming environment that is Python. The Python Package Index, also known as PyPI, is home to a sizable repository of open-source packages that programmers may utilize to easily incorporate third-party functionality into their projects. Knowledge-sharing, collaborative problem-solving, and continual learning are all encouraged and fostered by the use of online forums, coding communities, and social media platforms. In order to promote a culture that values expansion and innovation, conferences and meetings offer attendees the chance to engage with one another, discuss their experiences, and investigate newly emerging ideas.

Python's contribution to innovation is not limited to the programs it can run. Because of its versatility in rapid prototyping, experimentation can be carried out more quickly, which enables developers to quickly iterate and perfect their ideas. Because of its accessibility, Python has been instrumental in fostering interdisciplinary collaboration, which has led to the development of innovative projects involving researchers, designers, and engineers from a variety of professions. Python's flexibility places it at the front of a number of technological revolutions currently gathering steam, including the Internet of Things, quantum computing, and blockchain.

Python is constantly evolving in order to meet the ever-evolving requirements of software developers and the shifting technological world. Enhancements to the language address concerns such as performance and security while also harmonizing with modern paradigms of programming. Python's evolution from version 2 to version 3 was a watershed moment that exemplified the programming language's dedication to continuous improvement and responsiveness to user needs.

The development of Python mirrors the story of innovation, which is a narrative of enthusiasm, teamwork, and the transforming influence of new ideas. Because of its ease of use, even programming newbies may get started, yet the complexity of the language makes it appealing to seasoned programmers. Python's applicatuions may be found in a wide variety of fields and sectors, which exemplifies the language's ability to translate conceptual problems into workable solutions. Python's influence is prepared to extend further, enabling both rookie programmers beginning their coding journeys as well as experienced developers to construct complicated applications just as one stands on the edge of an increasingly dynamic technological future. Not only does Python gives individuals the ability to write code quickly, but it also gives one the ability to mould the world into one that is progressive, inclusive, and filled with limitless possibilities.

Made in the USA
Columbia, SC
25 October 2023

24932155R00057